Grantham
In the News

1951-1975

GRANTHAM
Journal

at heart  publications

Acknowledgements

Thanks to all the Journal reporters and photographers who recorded the town's activity during this quarter century.

Also thanks to the readers who allowed me to use their pictures, including:
Keith Harrison, Shirley Hind,
Elaine Lovegrove, Mike Matsell,
Stan Matthews, Peter Nicholls
and Chris Ward.

First published in 2007 by
At Heart Ltd, 32 Stamford Street, Altrincham,
Cheshire, WA14 1EY

in conjunction with
Grantham Journal, 46 High Street, Grantham, NG31 6NE

Images: Grantham Journal
Text: John Pinchbeck

Printed and bound by Bell & Bain Ltd., Glasgow

ISBN: 978-1-84547-141-5

Introduction

The third quarter of the 20th Century is an era that began with hope at the end of the war and finished with industrial strife, not just in Grantham but right across the country.

For Grantham, this was a time that saw the reconstruction and renewal of the post-war years completely alter the town, with many of the old attractive buildings giving way to new, indifferent designs. Steam locomotives, the cinema and a shop on every corner had also gone by the end of this period.

Grantham's engineering base also suffered. Names that had dominated the town for a century – Hornsby, Coultas, Grantham Boiler & Crank and the Loco – all disappeared. Even younger companies like Aveling Barford, BMARCo, Bjorlow and R H Neal began to flounder. In 1951, the town's engineering industry accounted for around 10,000 jobs. In 1975 it represented just a quarter of that.

But this town had its fair share of celebrations during this time. In the Sixties, the locals celebrated its 500th birthday by building an indoor swimming pool – eventually. And in the Seventies Margaret Thatcher, the daughter of a Grantham alderman, became leader of the Conservative party, later going on to become Britain's first woman prime minister.

This is the story of the Fifties, Sixties and half of the Seventies, told through the stories and experiences of people living in the area. They are real people, not just the nobility of the town and villages around, but also the poor and the lawbreakers.

For many people with Grantham connections, there is the added fun of knowing many of the people and incidents in the book. For anyone who has never even been to Grantham, it is a social history of any English town during the period.

Throughout there are lots of clues to the reality of life more than half a century ago, with an insight into the very different value of money back then. Decimalisation was introduced in this era, and appropriately all financial references have been converted into modern currency for a generation that will no longer understand guineas, half-crowns or fifteen-and-six.

It is not a book where you have to start at the beginning, but one for picking up and putting down any time.

John Pinchbeck
August 2007

1951 Grantham in the News

Farmers risk lives to free dead airman

THREE Cold Harbour men risked their lives trying to rescue an airman from a blazing aircraft.

Farmer Walter Jackson, his son Sidney (19) and farm worker Henry Frankish (25) saw the Mosquito crash into a field.

At great risk to themselves, they managed to pull one man out but he was found to be dead. A second body was found in the wreckage.

Both airmen were stationed at RAF Hemswell, near Gainsborough.

The plane got into difficulties over Grantham and black smoke was seen pouring from one engine.

It crashed into a ploughed field off the main Grantham-Donington Road. The tragedy happened shortly before a passing-out parade at nearby RAF Spitalgate.

Mr Sidney Jackson said: "The plane was flying low as if it wanted to land at Spitalgate. It came just over the treetops and was in flames as soon as it hit the ground.

"We knew they were in trouble so we drove to the scene in the car.

"We saw the poor fellow in the middle of the fire. His clothes were on fire. We pulled him out and pulled his clothes off bit by bit."

An inquest recorded death was caused by shock from severe burns.

Ammo found

SIXTY-eight rounds of stengun ammunition, found at Alma Park, were taken to Grantham police station by schoolboy Patrick Kilgallon, of Uplands Drive. Police warned gardeners in the area to be careful when digging.

Not Wednesday

TOWN traders overwhelmingly rejected a proposal to change early closing day from Thursdays to Wednesdays.

They said the only good reason for it was that planned power cuts always took place on Wednesdays.

Rally marred by heckler

A HUGE crowd turned out in Grantham Market Place to see Clement Atlee.

Mr Atlee, who was supporting Labour candidate Albert Millett, was the first serving Prime Minister in history to officially visit the town.

But just after he concluded his 20-minute speech, a heckler prevented Mr Millett from speaking.

After the heckler with a loud speaker shouted: "This is the voice of Liberalism", the hostile crowd turned on him and he had to be escorted by the police.

Mr Millett put on a gramophone record to drown out the intruder without success.

Mayor gives out prizes

MAYOR of Grantham, Susan Brace, presented the awards to children at Alma Park Church Sunday School. She took time to read one of the books to the children. With her was her Mayoress, the Hon Caroline Cust, daughter of Lord Brownlow.

Leaping fish

FRIED fish shot up 10 per cent from 3p per piece to 3.3p. This was the seventh increase since 1937. The minimum portion of chips remained 1¼p.

Keeping them rolling

SANITARY inspector Mr Taylor asked the public to save paper for recycling. He said it was needed to keep the paper mills rolling and to earn money towards the town's refuse collecting service.

Spot of bother

SCHOOLS remained closed in January due to an outbreak of measles. Borough medical officer Dr Ross said: "There is no need for alarm in view of the mild nature of the outbreak." There were 35 cases per week reported compared to 75 at the end of 1950.

Blanket increase

THE price of blankets shot through the roof, doubling last year's cost. One tradesman said he was selling them at £8.40 a pair but had sold out. "I could have sold 100 more," he said. "The outlook for cold winter nights is bleak – especially for newly-weds without a bottom drawer."

Elementary

TWO ex-King's School pupils who collected Sherlock Holmes stories, were consulted for an exhibition at 223b Baker Street, London.

Michael Pointer (24) and Tony Howlett had collect hundreds of books, photographs and cuttings and were recognised as authorities on Sir Arthur Conan Doyle's fictional character.

Continue to work

RAILWAYMEN decided to continue working despite saying they were dissatisfied with British Railways' pay offer.

At a meeting of ASLEF in the Labour Hall they said they were dismayed by the offer of 32.5p a week for cleaners and 57.5p for top rate drivers, bringing their weekly basic wage to £7.50 per week.

Dowsby farmer's idea

THE idea for radio soap opera The Archers was the brainchild of a Dowsby man.

Farmer Henry Burtt was meeting with BBC bosses to discuss farming programmes when he suggested a "farming Dick Barton".

Asked his opinion of the series which began last year, he said: "It is a most attractive programme which should appeal also to those not in agriculture."

Shop shuts for road widening

ANTIQUES shop T B Cooper was the first casualty in a road widening scheme at the foot of Watergate.

Town council workmen had already started demolishing the top of Watergate, to widen the Vine Street junction. Work also began on pulling down the narrow Chapel Street, cutting out the traffic bottleneck between Brook Street and Watergate.

Bishop's move

BISHOP of London, Dr J W C Wand, unveiled a memorial in 1951 in the Old School, Grantham King's School in memory of old boys killed in the Second World War.

An old boy himself, he was there for the school's Founders Day service.

Death of St Anne's vicar of 40 years

THE Rev Edwin Millard, Vicar of St Anne's Church, Grantham, for 40 years until his retirement through ill health, died at home.

He was 77.

One of a family of nine, Mr Millard, of Highfield, Cold Harbour Lane, was a vicar's son. He was the first vicar of St Anne's Church.

Known locally as 'Monkey' Millard, he kept a small zoo with kangaroos, lemurs, cranes and deer as well as monkeys.

A vegetarian, he edited an anti-blood sports magazine for children.

Much travelled, he was the first white man to visit Figig, 500km into the Sahara desert.

The funeral service at St Anne's Church was led by his brother Canon A H Millard and his successor, the Rev E E Jourdain.

Margaret to marry

MARGARET Roberts, daughter of former Mayor Alfred Roberts, celebrated the General Election by getting engaged.

Miss Roberts (26) fought Dartford for the Tories, cutting Labour's majority from 13,638 to 12,334.

The youngest woman candidate in the General Election, she announced her planned marriage to Denis Thatcher, a company director who was 10 years her senior.

Hero fireman is told his driver will receive the reward money

QUICK thinking by the Grantham crew on the footplate of an Edinburgh to King's Cross express saved what could have been one of the worst disasters in railway history.

The Heart of Midlothian left Grantham station with nearly 500 passengers and was negotiating a curve near Peterborough at 60mph when fireman J H Perkins spotted another train on the same line.

He alerted driver E Walton (64), of Robertson Road.

Mr Walton said: "For a brief second I was numb."

He brought the 500-tonne train to a standstill less than a dozen metres from the obstructing fish train. British Railways rewarded the driver for his alertness.

He was presented with a £2.10 reward by Eastern Region superintendent J Blundell. Mr Blundell said the fish train should not have been on the line, blaming a "signalling irregularity".

He said he was sorry there was no award for the part fireman Perkins (31), of West View, Ancaster, played but his name would be passed to a higher authority.

Mr Walton said: "I want nothing like it again. It shook me."

Numbers up

THE census revealed Grantham's population had grown by 3,694 over 20 years.

The total of 23,405 was made up of 11,239 men and 12,166 women.

Time off for tates

THERE were 17,989 schooldays lost by 1,278 Kesteven children helping with the potato harvest.

Education director Dr T W P Golby said attendance in Kesteven was 88.7 per cent.

Swan upping

THREE swans fought a bloody battle in Wyndham Park bathing pool. One was covered in blood and died a week later.

Little gangsters

THREE brothers aged 9, 10 and 13 were each given a year's probation by Grantham Juvenile Court for stealing seven rat traps.

The youngest also admitted stealing 40 cigarettes, a ring and a packet of cocoa. Magistrate Mrs A. Barford said: "You are just little gangsters.

"Had I done such a thing when I was a child, I would have had such a beating, I couldn't have sat down for a week."

Top Tory in Town

MP Anthony Eden caught the train back to London following a major speech in Nottingham.

He had addressed 6,000 members of the Conservative Party faithful, before staying the night at Hawksworth Manor.

There he was a guest of Ald and Mrs Armitage.

Picture shows Mr Eden with Station Master Mr Scampion (left) and Grantham Conservative agent Stanley Hodgkins.

Chance of cable TV

REDIFFUSION (East Midlands) asked Grantham Town Council's permission to dig up streets to lay wiring for radio and TV.

The network company said there would be a choice of three radio stations as well as television.

Councillors were lukewarm about the idea, saying it would lead to many overhead wires. Radio would cost 15p per week but TV was much more expensive.

Unfortunately the scheme was not approved.

Central shuts down

THE Central Cinema, High Street, closed its doors for the last time.

The final film was Slatery's Hurricane. The hall doubled as a corn exchange on Saturdays and farmers were stunned to hear it was closing. Local National Farmers Union chairman E A Toplis said: "It came as a complete surprise to us when we were told."

It was said to have been bought by Lyons for a provisions store.

Grantham in the News 1952

Another fine mess you've gotten us into

HOLLYWOOD superstars Stan Laurel and Oliver Hardy were given a five-star welcome when they opened the Chamber of Trade's three-day exhibition at the Guildhall.

After lunch at the Red Lion Hotel, High Street, they were greeted by hundreds of fans at the Guildhall.

The antics of the pair had the crowd roaring with laughter.

Laurel tousled his hair and looked sorrowful while Hardy flipped his tie in the style he made his own.

The speechmaking was continually held up by the pair's antics at the top of the Guildhall steps. Even Olga Healey and her husband Bill, of Bottesford, Laurel's sister and brother-in-law, laughed as Stanley tried to attract Hardy's attention to tell him "you're standing on my foot."

John Foster of the chamber, thanked the pair and commended the exhibitors, officials and committee.

At the comedians' request, the chamber made a donation to the Ancient Order of Water Rats, showbiz's benevolent fund.

Cheers! Let's raise a glass to New Year

BIG-hearted magistrates allowed the public to drink the New Year in for the first time since the First World War.

They allowed pubs to open until 12.15am on New Year's Day.

They also extended closing time from 10pm to 11pm on Christmas Eve and Boxing Day.

The decision went against the recommendation of Grantham Police.

Insp Cox said he saw no good reason why New Year's Eve drinking should go beyond 11pm.

Solicitor John Norton, for the Licensed Vituallers Association, said he hoped it would not be abused.

Grantham brewery in merger

LOCAL brewers Mowbray and Company merged with J W Green of Luton which controlled 687 licensed premises.

The effect was said to increase Grantham's importance as a brewing centre and production was planned to increase.

Mowbray and Co, which had 204 houses, was founded in 1828 and became a public company in 1880.

The brewery had premises on London Road, Rycroft Street and Brewery Hill.

Turned on

ELECTRICITY was connected to homes in Turnor Crescent homes after 54 tenants agreed. Eight were against and one failed to reply.

Leg operation

QUEEN'S Park Rangers inside forward Cyril Hatton, from Grantham, underwent a knee operation for an injury received on Boxing Day 1951.

Bombs away

AN RAF disposal unit announced a team had swept Alma Park for ammunition and was certified free of explosives.

Rise for mayor

THE mayor's remuneration was increased from £250 to £350, the first rise since 1945.

New names

NEW roads in the Princess Drive area were called Queensway, Ash Grove, Almond Grove and Cornwall Close.

Lighting up

ELECTRIC street lighting was installed on Harlaxton Road, between Earlesfield Lane and Springfield Road.

HEAVY OAK REPRO SUITE

4ft. 6in. Dresser	£27 16 9
Table	£14 0 0
4 Chairs ....each	£3 8 9

Can be purchased separately or completes as a suite for £56 1s 9d.

JOHN HALL & SON Ltd.

42 ST. PETER'S HILL   GRANTHAM

Tea for Indians

HOUSEWIVES in the Gonerby Hill Foot area set up a table at the end of Cliffe Road to make tea for Indian seamen.

The 16 merchant sailors were stranded when their coach was in collision with another bus taking the City of Glasgow Police Pipe Band home from a French tour.

The ladies intervened as the 16 Indians were waiting to be taken to hospital, many suffering facial injuries after being thrown from their seats.

None of the Scottish policemen were injured.

Had his chips

ONE of Yorkshire's best known fish and chip shops, formerly owned by Harry Ramsden, was bought by Grantham fish frier Bill Kirby for £35,000, as a present for his son Gordon.

He said he planned to sell his London Road business, which he had run for 16 years, to help his son at the new venture in Guiseley.

New use

THE town council announced it had no use for Grantham's bomb sites for building council houses.

A committee was asked to deal with them.

Old theatre makes way for garage

A LINK with the town's theatrical history ended when the old billiards saloon, in Swinegate, was pulled down to make way for a filling station.

The building on the corner of Brook Street, owned by Lou Musson, who also owned the new Empire Garage next door, had a varied history.

A wedding was celebrated there in 1876, when it was used as a Wesleyan Chapel.

Built in 1800, the building also had been a theatre, a gymnasium, a sale room, a meeting room, a billiard hall, and most recently a warehouse for a vegetable wholesaler.

We get too much says schoolboy

A TWELVE-year-old Grantham boy admitted he earned too much money.

In a survey into pocket money received by local children, Michael Winfield, of New Street, said he thought 25p a week was about right.

He said: "I earn 35p a week. It's too much. I give half of it to my mother."

King's School headmaster W J Huggins said: "Boarders at our school get 12.5p per week. Many children are paid too much in my opinion."

Headteacher E W Jacobs at the Boys' Central School said: "I consider 10p is about right. That would pay for a weekly visit to the cinema and leave plenty for sweets."

Miss Nina Hewitt at the Girls' Central said pocket money was not necessary. "Most girls are on friendly terms with their mothers. They manage to get money when they need it."

Earlesfield housing in focus

THE next area for housing development would be in Earlesfield, between Dysart Road and the Grantham Canal, Grantham housing committee announced.

The Harrowby end of town would be exhausted by 1956 so work was planned to begin on a sewerage system for Earlesfield within a year, to be ready in time.

Alderman Goodliff reads the proclamation in the Market Place

Pensions Introduced

A PENSION scheme for male manual workers was introduced at Ruston and Hornsby. The £70,000 annual cost was borne by the company.

At 65 the employees had the option of taking £55 a year pension or £150 cash and a smaller pension. Male employees were eligible to join after five years' service.

Villagers regain cup

BOTTESFORD won the Thompson Cup for the second time in three years.

Ruston and Hornsby bowler Jack Macartney suffered a series of dropped catches.

A crowd of 2,500 turned out at Grantham's London Road ground to watch.

King George VI dies

ALDERMAN William Goodliff, Mayor of Grantham, read the proclamation of King George VI's death in 1952. It had first been read outside the Guildhall, where thousands of schoolchildren lined up to hear the news.

As a mark of respect, all functions at Aveling Barford social club were suspended between the death of King George VI and his burial. Grantham Technical College Students' Association committee also postponed all planned events during the period of mourning.

Denis' dogs on death row

TWO St Bernard dogs, one owned by former Grantham MP Denis Kendall, the other formerly his, were ordered to be put down by Grantham Magistrates. The order came after evidence that the dogs, each worth up to £300, were worrying sheep in Belton Park and frightened several people. Mr Kendall said the sentence was "vicious".

He said: "They are friendly but don't like other dogs."

Gamekeeper Arthur Ghent said 15 lambs had been found dead with total casualties being 40.

Royal visit

THE Princess Royal paid a visit to Grantham in her role as Commandant-in-Chief of the British Red Cross.

She inspected units from South Lincolnshire in Wyndham Park where 800 people took part.

They paraded their new colours which were dedicated by the Bishop of Lincoln in St Wulfram's Church.

Band told to pipe down

GRANTHAM Carnival Band was told to pipe down at rehearsals.

The town council told them they would have to rehearse more quietly if bookings at the Westgate Hall were to continue.

A nearby resident said: "On one occasion recently, the noise of certain instruments was terrific. The walls were vibrating."

Secretary Mr R W Handley said: "The only alternative is to go out of town to train. We've had two offers but both are attached to pubs so we couldn't take children there."

He said the band, which began in May with six members, had since increased to 40.

Two lorries in collision near airfield

A VEHICLE carrying 3,600 gallons of petrol was in a collision at Somerby crossroads, near RAF Spitalgate airfield.

The other lorry carried steel girders which were spilled across the road blocking it for several hours.

Neither driver was seriously hurt although their lorries were write-offs.

Freedom for airmen

THOUSANDS of spectators turned out on St Peter's Hill to watch the freedom of the borough ceremony for RAF Spitalgate.

The privilege entitles the airmen to march through the town with colours flying, bands playing, drums beating and bayonets fixed.

Club on the brink

GRANTHAM FC was tottering on the brink. Directors opened a recovery fund with a £2,500 target. Aveling Barford and BMARCo put up £100 each, while John Lee and Henry Bell gave £5 each. A pub-to-pub collection raised £20.

The club referred to a "run of disaster" of illness and injuries to players putting the club in a precarious league position. It continued: "We now feel we must turn to local business houses and ask them for financial aid to keep the club going.

"It can be done by donation or buying shares."

House auction

A FREEHOLD property, 11 Commercial Road, was sold at Golding's auction with vacant possession for £550.

Poor turnout

GRANTHAM FC's smallest crowd on record defied a blizzard to watch them beat Denaby 2-0.

Only 444 spectators watched the Midland League match at London Road.

Denis goes

FORMER Grantham MP, Denis Kendall, left town for the USA.

He was appointed general manager of the Mack Truck organisation, with an office at the Empire State Building, New York.

Drunkenness rises

SUPT W Ford told the borough licensing court drunkenness was on the increase.

He said: "In spite of the co-operation of licensees and supervision by police, 24 persons were arrested for drunkenness last year."

This compared with seven in 1946, eight in 1948 and 23 in 1950.

Grantham in the News 1953

The Mayor's parade the following Sunday saw much better weather

CHILDREN from Edward Street, see at Wesleyan Chapel rooms, Bridge End Road, celebrated the Queen's Coronation.

Coronation celebrations washed out by weather

WINTRY winds and driving rain marred the June celebrations for the Coronation of Queen Elizabeth II.

The carnival in the afternoon was a near washout, with few people watching.

The parade was headed by the Young Farmers' Club with Queen Elizabeth I on horseback.

Ruston and Hornsby's band followed, then came the Carnival Queen, Anne Geddes, with her attendants.

Trade floats were won by Fosters Builders, followed by Co-op Milk and F P Selby, wood merchant.

GPO Telephones won the senior section, followed by Grantham Legion and Grantham Co-op Society and Women's Guild. The juniors prizes went to Grantham YMCA, Harrowby Youth Centre and Grantham League of Hospital Friends. At a special children's day, 12,000 sandwiches were prepared together with 4,500 jellies and blancmanges.

The food was distributed around the town's schools.

The streets were a mass of colour with the return of community spirit. Alford Street won with Cowes Road second and Buckminster Gardens in third place.

Work starts on estate

A START was made on building hundreds of new council homes as the town got closer to Belton Park. Pictured is the new road, Princess Drive, being surfaced at the junction with Belton Lane.

Air force chiefs say call it 'Spitalgate' not 'Spittlegate'

IT'S RAF Spitalgate – and that's official. The Air Ministry said new maps will not change the name, even though it admits it is wrong.

A spokesman said: "From researches by the Air Ministry, it seems clear that 'Spittlegate' is the usage of antiquity and can be traced to 1553, although in modern times 'Spitalgate' has also been adopted."

Steps were taken to alter the spelling following a visit by Viscount Sandon, of the Royal Commission of Historical Manuscripts.

But air force bosses were unmoved. The spokesman said: "In the charter conferred upon the station, to signal freedom of entry into Grantham, the spelling is recorded as 'Spitalgate'. It has been decided the order to change the name shall be withdrawn."

Council road rage

WEST Kesteven Rural District Council condemned the proposed Long Bennington bypass, backing the parish council.

A spokesman said it was: "an absolute waste of money and good food producing land.

"The road through the village can be made adequate and safe for traffic and pedestrians at a comparatively small cost."

Girls demand proper jobs

BOYS were looking towards apprenticeships in engineering when they left school, according to the town's Youth Employment Officer. Others went into farming at Caythorpe Court Farm Institute.

But a third of girls went into shops and a third into offices.

Miss C H Silvester said clerical work did not appeal to boys. She said there is not enough office jobs for the girls wanting work.

She said: "There are odd cases of girls staying at home to help their mothers but the trend now is towards going to work.

"Domestic helps are on the decline and girls going into service want jobs as mothers' helps."

"Generally, young folk want a job in town and do not want to travel away from home."

Firemen tackle wood mill blaze from windows

COTTAGERS in Wharf Road were forced to leave their homes when a blaze ripped through a builders' yard. Joinery mills containing expensive machinery and finished products were blazing out of control within minutes of first being spotted.

Neighbours helped each other remove furniture in case the fire continued to spread with the help of the stiff wind. Firemen entered three of the cottages and trained their hoses from upstairs windows on to the inferno.

About 1,000sq m of mill and shop were destroyed but the cause of the fire was never found.

Denton Parish Church's organ had been stored in the mill until only hours earlier having just had repairs completed.

But windows, doors and a cocktail bar for a local pub were destroyed.

Secret Royal visit

THE Queen stayed in Leadenham overnight – and most of the villagers were unaware.

She was on the royal train which pulled into a siding alongside the Grantham-Lincoln line at midnight and left just after 7am. The Duke of Edinburgh and Princess Margaret were also on board. The Royal party was on its way to Edinburgh for the January wedding of the Earl of Dalkeith to Jane McNeill.

Browned off

LORD Brownlow threatened to close Belton Park to the public after the gardens were damaged by vandals.

The latest act was a veranda near the lily pond being thrown into the lake while shutters were torn from the boathouse windows.
He said: "I'm weary and disgusted.

Gone off pop

CORONATION festivities at Barkestone-le-Vale ended with a bang – literally.

The firework display finished quickly. The first one was lit, causing the rest to go off.

New clear power

GAS lighting in Dudley Road was replaced by electricity at a cost of £400.

Last bus home

LINCOLNSHIRE Road Car was asked by the borough council to provide a bus service between 10pm and 10.30pm from the town to Tennyson Avenue.

This was to allow people to bus home after attending places of amusement.

Strike-breaking keeper is sent to Coventry

GRANTHAM FC goalkeeper Ron Hewitt hit the national headlines by being sent to Coventry by workmates.

He suffered the angry silence at Staveley Ironworks, near Chesterfield, when he went to work during the national engineers' strike.

The following Saturday, when Grantham played Notts County Reserves at Meadow Lane, Hewitt was barracked by the home supporters.

They chanted slogans such as "Send him to Coventry" and "Scab, scab, scab".

And the County players were equally hostile during the match, slamming four goals past him without reply.

Who has stolen our dojo?

GRANTHAM Judo Club's headquarters disappeared after thieves drove it away on the lorry.

The club bought the 20m x 6m wooden building from RAF Harlaxton, Gorse Lane, to be their dojo.

But when they went to collect the hut, it wasn't there.

Club secretary and Springfield Road barber Arthur Jones was furious at the disappearance.

He said: "If we find the culprits we'll give them a memorable course in judo."

One of the best

GRANTHAM'S busy bus station was regarded as one of the best in the country. The vehicles entered from St Catherine's Road and made their exit on to St Peter's Hill. Facilities included covered shelters, and a popular canteen.

Village women produce hate list

MEMBERS of Ingoldsby WI told their men which chores they hated most at one of their meetings. These included skinning rabbits, cleaning flues, black-leading grates and plucking geese. But one member had no complaints, saying household duties had to be done.

Doctor sends children to seaside

DR Charles Frier, who set up his first Grantham practice in 1896, is pictured in Avenue Road sending underprivileged children to Skegness, thanks to a fund he set up.

Dr Frier's Holiday Fund for Crippled Children became the major local charity.

Mr Parfitt, in uniform, was the NSPCC inspector and his wife, wearing glasses, is fourth right from him.

In front of Mr Parfitt, wearing a hat, is Amy Coles, who was matron in charge.

The Mayor and Mayoress on the right of the picture is Stanley Foster and his wife.

Dr Frier's practice was at Spittlegate House, London Road.

Council to buy Alma Park for £17,500

GRANTHAM Borough Council was set to buy the Alma Park estate – nicknamed Heartbreak Corner – following complaints by tenants about conditions. The houses – built in the First World War as an army barracks and later used to house prisoners-of-war, was Government-owned.

The estate was regarded as a clearance area, from which the council select its own tenants.

Flu bug bites

SCHOOLS were hit by a flu bug which cut attendances of many schools to 70 per cent, while some classes were halved. Staff as well as children were affected.

Bricks run out

HOUSE building came to an end for three months after materials ran out.

Builders had to wait between six and eight months after placing orders for their bricks and the supply of cement dried up altogether.

Thorny slip

GRANTHAM cricketers slipped up when Yorkshire and England opening bat Herbert Sutcliffe opened the club's pavilion at the London Road ground. Roses decorating the table before him were red – the emblem of rival county Lancashire.

Dutch master

CANON L A Arendzen (80) retired after 40 years at St Mary's Roman Catholic Church, North Parade. A painter of great ability, he was the son of an eminent Dutch etcher.

During his time there, he raised thousands of pounds for St Mary's by selling his own paintings.

You can't beat milk

BROWN Brothers went hi-tech by introducing the latest technology at their dairy. After supplying milk to their customers from metal churns for many years, and using ladles to fill the housewives' jugs, they installed a bottling plant at their Manthorpe dairy.

The tops of these milk bottles were cardboard discs which schoolboys used for playing 'milkies'. Each of Brown Brothers' floats carried the slogan "You may whip our cream but you can't beat our milk."

Cyril's the new boss

GRANTHAM FC signed Cyril Hatton as player-manager from Chesterfield. He had lived in Grantham for most of his life, even when playing for Notts County, Queens Park Rangers and Chesterfield.

An FA coach, he twice represented the Football Association.

He said: "I have always looked on Grantham as my home. I want to see us go places."

Hatton was only the second player-manager engaged by the club. The first was Harry Pringle, in the 1930s.

A gate of 3,658 watched Hatton's first match in August, although his team lost 2-1 to Nottingham Forest Reserves.

Child hurt in taxi ride

A CHILD on her way to Goldsmith Road by taxi, was injured when she fell out after the door opened unexpectedly.

She was one of two in the cab returning from Doncaster. The incident happened on Station Road.

She was taken to Grantham Hospital where she received several stitches before being released.

The taxi driver of Oak Drive, Alma Park, was fined £1 with 80p costs for failing to report an accident.

Legless man saved from the scaffold

A MAN who threw himself under a train, at Gonerby Hill Foot, severing both legs, was sentenced to death at Lincoln Assizes for murder.

John Docherty (28) was carried away by a warder after hearing his fate At a three minute hearing, he admitted murdering his ex-fiancee Sibyl Hoy, of Co Durham, in the grounds of Arnoldfield.

He stabbed her 19 times with a butchers' knife. After the offence, Docherty ran to the railway line and threw himself under the King's Cross-Edinburgh express severing both legs.

Mr Justice Barry told him: "There is only one possible course open to this court."

His sentence was commuted to life imprisonment by Home Secretary Sir David Maxwell-Fyfe as he was unable to walk to the scaffold.

Thunderbolt

EIGHT Kerry Hill sheep owned by Lord Brownlow were killed by lightning in one of the worst storms for many years. They were part of a 900 flock at Belton Park.

Their value was put at £50.

Elaine's blow for women

ELAINE Harris, of Station Road, Grantham, struck a blow for women musicians. The 15-year-old joined the top all-women Ivy Benson Band, playing at Torquay.

She saw the band playing at the Marble Arch Corner House, London, and asked if she could have an audition. After hearing Elaine play, Miss Benson signed her on immediately.

Elaine began playing cornet when she was eight and for two years studied piano under King's School music master Stephen Mundy.

She also played trumpet in the Grantham Orchestra and Ruston and Hornsby Band.

Waterproof secret claim sinks in the High Court

THE secret process that made suede waterproof could not be protected by law.

Bjorlow (Great Britain) tried to prevent former employee Ronald Minter from passing on the secret.

But the hearing in the High Court Chancery Division for a restraining injunction was rejected.

The process was known only to a handful of past and present employees including Mr Minter, of Caythorpe.

His counsel, Mervyn Davies, said the process was not a secret but a skilled method of applying known chemicals.

The action was thrown out although Bjorlow was given right of appeal.

Signalling success

GRANTHAM was one of the busiest railway towns in the country, according to stationmaster Mr H Scampion.

He said on one day in the year, 434 trains were signalled past the Grantham North box, which contained 105 levers. He said the box was the most up-to-date outside London.

Cheap rates

LINCOLNSHIRE Road Car announced a special workman's fare of 3p from Alma Park gates to the town centre.

Bomb death

PORTER Lewis Webb (52) was killed while loading bombs at Bottesford station. He was struck by an RAF 13-tonne crane which reversed into him as he was helping to load bombs into the wagons.

Called to the bar

MARGARET Thatcher (27) daughter of former Mayor Alfred Roberts, of North Parade, Grantham, was called to the bar.

Based in Chelsea, she became one of the few women to join the select band of female barristers.

Driver retires

ENGINE driver Matthew Hudson (centre) retired in 1954 after 50 years, 25 of them as a main line driver. He drove both King George VI and Winston Churchill.

Council tells kids to ignore the law

A PLAYING field ban on cricket and football was condemned by town councillors.

They said notices banning both sports at either end of Stonebridge Close, off Avenue Road, were a nonsense. Grantham MP Joe Godber asked the council to look into it after a petition against the ban was handed to him by residents.

Coun Joseph Hardaker said: "Although signs were put up, we have no intention of stopping children playing our national sports. The notice refers to adults not children."

But Ald Rothwell Lee said it encouraged children to snub the law. He said: "If that is the case, the notices ought to be amended to say children only.

"It is not wise for children to play contrary to the notices put up. It encourages breaking the law."

Spooky service

MYSTERIOUS noises interrupted a service at St Peter's Hill Congregational Church.

Several times the Rev T S Key had to pause as the spooky noises tried to bring proceedings to a halt.

The noise was described as a mixture of gurgling water and flapping wings.

Afterwards, stewards investigated but found nothing.

"We're baffled," said one of them. "I don't think we'll ever know what it was."

Pubs get extra time for soccer match

MAGISTRATES decided the Lincolnshire Senior Cup final between Grantham FC and Boston was a big occasion.

They said drinkers at London Road pubs Blue Horse and Barley Mow could enjoy and extra hour drinking, from 3pm to 4pm on the match day. They turned down a similar request from the Reaper and Reindeer on the grounds they were too far from the ground – even though the Reaper was only two doors away from the Blue Horse.

Afterward, magistrate George Mills said league matches did not constitute a special occasion.

Applications were only considered by pubs close to the London Road ground.

He said: "We don't want to hinder a man getting a drink at half-time."

The Fleet's in

THE Royal Navy held an exhibition in the paddock, off Avenue Road – formally known as Stonebridge Close – with a giant model of the aircraft carrier Triumph. It was a big hit with the children.

In the background is Pidcock's Maltings which ran the length of Welham Street from Avenue Road to East Street.

Tyre fire fails to close Vacu-Lug factory

A £50,000 blaze ripped through Vacu-Lug Traction's Gonerby Hill Foot factory

But prompt work by firefighters saved the works from closure.

The 60-strong workforce at the main factory went on staggered shifts and was back to normal within a month.

The cause remained a mystery.

Final days of Empire

THE Empire Theatre (above) closed its doors for the last time.

Built as a theatre, in George Street in Victorian times, with a stage door in East Street, it had shown films before the purpose-built cinemas arrived.

At one time it had been the meeting place for the Salvation Army.

In its later days, it became a cinema only, showing old films with a price range from 5p downstairs to 10p in the circle.

Car saving

THE Chief Constable of Lincolnshire stopped delivery of all new patrol cars, saying the present vehicles should last for at least 100,000km.

He demanded better maintenance and cut his order down to four new patrol cars at £245 each.

New contract

GRANTHAM Borough Council accepted a tender from Selleck Nicholls, of St Austell, Cornwall, to build 52 Cornish unit houses, near Edinburgh Road and north of Queensway.

The total cost was £73,699.89.

Font moved

THE font from the demolished St James's Church, East Allington, was presented to the rebuilt St Michael's Church, Waddington, which was bombed in the war.

More to swim

SEASON tickets for children using Dysart Park and Wyndham Park swimming baths were increased from 30p to 37.5p a year, the first increase since 1946.

The foundation stone is laid at the Church of the Ascension, Edinburgh Road

Work starts on church and school

THE foundation stone was laid by Lord Brownlow. for the new Church of the Ascension, on Edinburgh Road. It replaced the wooden building on New Beacon Road.

The new church cost £10,000.

A sealed copper cylinder was buried beneath the foundation stone. It contained a copy of St Wulfram's parish magazine, a copy of the order of stone-laying service and a scroll naming the volunteers who prepared the site.

Cash for the new brick-built church, which doubled as a community centre, came from the sale of St Saviour's Church.

The foundation stone of St Saviour's, Manners Street, was laid in 1880 by Countess Brownlow.

Work also began on the new secondary school off Harrowby Lane to accommodate 650 children.

It would be called St Wulfram's School.

Mac calls it a day

GRANTHAM FC goal ace Jack Macartney retired from Midland League Football after 18 years with Grantham. He took over as player coach for the reserves.

The scorer of 500 goals for his club, he said: "I can't go on forever." He netted 53 times in 1946/47 and 52 the following season. He also slammed a club record eight past Bradford Park Avenue in Grantham's 9-6 victory on April 10, 1948.

Grantham in the News 1955

Ice cream man goes bananas

THE driver of an ice cream van had a lucky escape on the Broad Street/North Street junction when his van overturned following a collision. The other vehicle involved was a lorry carrying bananas. The road was blocked for two hours. No one was hurt. The corner shop belonged to former alderman Alfred Roberts

94-year-old spinster takes on intruder

GERTRUDE Hardwick was awakened in her Avenue Road home in the early hours of the morning, so she went downstairs to investigate.

Hearing a scream upstairs, she was met by her housekeeper who said there was an intruder.

The housekeeper said the man said he would not harm them as long as they didn't switch on the light.

Defiant Miss Hardwick switched on the lights and told the man to come downstairs. He obeyed her and as he left the house, he said: "I'm sorry I disturbed you."

Miss Harwick replied: "God bless you. Don't do it again."

The thief stole an apron and a handkerchief, a total value of 33p

Pen & cash for gang

BUNGLING burglars blew open two safes with gelignite at Grantham Co-op, St Peter's Hill – making off with £3 and a fountain pen.

They were disturbed before tackling the other four safes which contained most of the money.

The crime was particularly audacious as it was less than 100m from the police station.

Bus topped

EDITH Schofield (67) of 137 Alexandra Road, was struck on the head by a bus stop sign, which was knocked down by a passing car. She was taken to hospital for treatment but not detained.

Never on Sunday

SHOPKEEPER Vera Harris, of Harrowby Lane, was fined 50p for selling a jar of jam on a Sunday.

She had denied the charge.

Gasworks blaze peril

TWO 16-metre high scrubbing towers caught fire at Grantham Gasworks, Harlaxton Road.

Firemen pumped 100,000 litres of water from the canal to stop toxic chemicals blowing across the town. The fire was caused by demolition workers using oxy-acetylene cutters.

Mildew in town homes

TENANTS of the centre houses in blocks of four on Cherry Orchard, were suffering from the damp.

Coun Ron Briggs complained that although there had been no similar reports elsewhere, the mildew on those houses was plain to see.

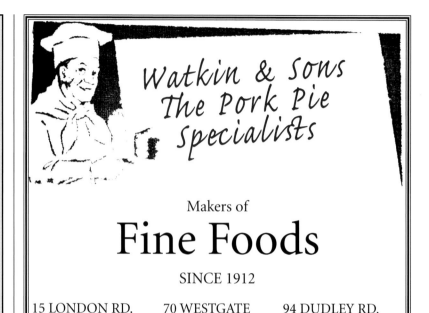
Barrowby Road bridge closed for 30 hours for urgent repairs

BARROWBY Road Railway Bridge was replaced in 30 hours. It was described by experts as the most delicate structural engineering job the town had seen.

The contract, which cost £10,000, began with the railway lines being torn up and the old bridge cut and removed by two giant cranes.

The cranes were soon lifting replacement steelwork into place. The Grantham-Nottingham road was closed for 12 hours while trains were either diverted or halted at Nottingham where passengers continued their journeys by bus.

Stuffed birds and eggs left in will

IN his will, the late Capt John Sharrard Reeve, of Leadenham House, left unsettled estate worth £22,648 net. Duty paid was £5,312. Probate was granted to his widow, his son and his daughter.

He left the county museum two cabinets of birds' eggs, a smaller cabinet of birds' skins and a collection of stuffed birds. Chauffeur, Mr H Cook, was left £300 if still in service or £50 if not.

Lost teeth shouting

A MAN working on an excavator lost his false teeth shouting instructions to a workmate. They slid under the machine and were crushed. He was granted a free replacement by Kesteven Health Committee.

Mayor is banned from Guildhall

GRANTHAM Mayor Ernest Hardy arrived at the Guildhall one evening only to be told: "You can't go in."
It happened when Boots hired the ballroom for its staff dance, with proceeds in aid of Dr Frier's Holiday Fund for Crippled Children.

Music was provided by the New Olympians.

Tickets were a sell-out and doormen were under strict instructions to refuse further entry.

Fortunately, one of the organisers spotted Mr Hardy being turned away and decided to 'make an exception in the circumstances'.

Heaven's above – it's the parson

THE Rev Jack Talent climbs the scaffold at the Church of the Epiphany, Earlesfield, which was nearing completion.

Drinking up crime fine

TWO police officers on duty after midnight tried the door of the Plough Inn, Welby Street, and found it unlocked.

When they went inside, they saw the landlord still serving whisky to three Irishmen in the smoke room. The three men said they were entitled to drink as they had paid 32½p each for a night's bed and board.

But when police checked the register, their names were not listed.

The licensee was fined a total of £20 on three charges of serving drinks after hours and one of failing to keep a register of people staying at the inn.

The Irishmen were each fined £2 for drinking out of hours.

Garage owner's wife is killed in stock car race

A GRANTHAM stock car driver was killed in a race at Coventry stadium after crashing into a barrier and being crushed by the steering wheel.

Agnes Hodgkins, the wife of Watergate garage owner J H Hodgkins, had been racing for about a year.

Her husband was competing in the same race.

Mrs Hodgkins, 28, was leading at the time of the accident.

She is believed to have misjudged the corner and ploughed into the barrier erected to protect spectators.

It was her first race at Coventry.

Born in Liverpool, she met her husband at Leicester speedway track. They had a three-year-old daughter called Bubbles.

It was the sport's first fatality since it was introduced to Britain the previous year.

Woodrow Wyatt campaigning for Labour in Market Place.

Parson fails to woo voters

JOE Godber retained the Grantham seat for the Conservatives at the General Election.

He polled 24,188 votes against Woodrow Wyatt (Labour) with 21,813, a majority of 2,375.

The Rev R C Gaul, Liberal's Fighting Parson, attracted only 1,624 votes and lost his deposit. He had to resign from the church to fight the election.

Mr Wyatt said afterwards: "We have lit the fire in the Grantham constituency which will not be put out. We shall return and so will a Labour Government."

Award for bird rescue

THREE Grantham firefighters were presented with awards after rescuing a pigeon.

C W Howkins, D. Nowell and T. Hoy of Kesteven Fire Service climbed the 30m St John's Church tower to rescue the bird caught up in wire.

Their gallantry led to the commendation by the RSPCA.

Mr H White of the animal charity said: "We do not give these certificates lightly."

Cut price rise says barber

ERNEST Hardy, a life member of the local branch of the National Hairdressers' Federation quit in protest at a new minimum charge. He objected to the price leap from 7½p to 10p.

Secretary Harry Mitchum said the decision to increase was made at a meeting attended by six of the 10 members.

Since then, one had reduced his price to 9p, another resigned and a third refused to put up his price.

Caught at court

SOLICITOR Ronald Tinkler, of Grantham, was fined £1 for causing an obstruction by parking his car in Sleaford while appearing at the town's magistrates' court.

Station closed

BARKSTON station was closed as part of British Railways' cost cutting.

Stationmaster F W Adams complained: "People seem to prefer the bus these days."

Dance hall plan

GRANTHAM Theatres, which bought the Empire, George Street, in December 1954, announced plans to turn it into a first-class ballroom.

The former cinema and theatre had the largest floor area of any building in town. The plans were abandoned later.

Fair exchange

TOWN councillors agreed to move the Mid-Lent Fair from the Market Place and Westgate.

The scheme fell through as they could find no viable or large enough alternative site.

Town ladies on visit to Parliament

MEMBERS of Grantham Townswomen's Guild about to board the train at the railway station, on their way to London for a visit to the House of Commons. This was followed by a tour of the Ideal Home Exhibition at Olympia.

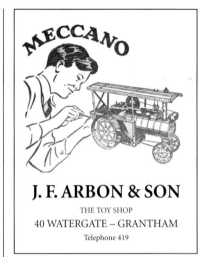

Bride and groom total 150 years

AFTER waiting 74 years before finally tying the knot, bachelor boy Thomas Moor, finally got married at Commercial Road Methodist Church.

The blushing bride was widow Edith Staniland, of Barracks Square, two years his senior.

They were the oldest bride and groom in Grantham for many years.

The couple had known each other since they grew up together in New Street. Best man was Salvationist Ben Coldron while matron of honour was Mrs J Hughes, 74, of Great Gonerby. She was given away by Mr Hughes, 76.

The couple made their home at Mr Moor's house in Bridge End Road.

Schools for new estate

TWO schools opened in the town, as building expanded in the Queensway area.

St Wulfram's Secondary School was opened by the Bishop of Lincoln, the Rt Rev Kenneth Riches.

The £142,579 three-storey building was designed to take 600 boys and girls.

Most new pupils were drawn from the National Schools in Castlegate and senior boys from Spitalgate School, Stonebridge, St Catherine's Road.

Earlier in the year, Belton Lane Primary School was opened by Lord Ancaster.

It cost £77,000.

Pipped at post

GRANTHAM were pipped into runners up spot by Newark, in the Round Table annual canoe race on the Grantham Canal.

Tight-fisted traders play Scrooge for Christmas

GRANTHAM tradesmen cancelled Father Christmas' visit to Grantham.

The mean shopkeepers also killed off the chance for festive illuminations. They said they were no longer interested in supporting Santa's annual visit.

A statement from Grantham Chamber of Trade said 180 members were asked to support a visit to town by Santa Claus. Only 30 agreed to take part.

The previous year Santa gave free lollies on his tour of the town by carriage and children had a half day off school. It cost each trader £2.

Chairman John Porter said: "This is a very poor show." Only 18 turned out to discuss Christmas illuminations, so the project was abandoned.

Of the 420 questionnaires sent to members with stamped addressed envelopes, 308 did not reply.

Only 43 people said they were interested in a Christmas lighting scheme, while 53 said they were not.

Tailor Colin Tipler said: "It's a farce when only this low number turn out to discuss something that was of value to the town."

The scheme would have cost £1,400.

Big Freeze bites hard

GRANTHAM was in the grip of a big freeze, but plenty of youngsters enjoyed it. These schoolboys pictured were enjoying a February afternoon on the Grantham Canal.

Behind them is the area known as 'The Willows' which were grown as osier beds by WB Harrison in Victorian times.

Healthy town

THE town medical officer reported one case of pulmonary tuberculosis, three of scarlet fever and one puerperal pyrexia.

Schools reported two cases of chicken pox, one of scarlet fever and one of ringworm.

Foggy, foggy do

FOG cut Grantham FC's gate at London Road, to a disappointing 1,280 – the season's lowest Midland League gate. Twice that year the crowd topped 3,000 including 3,867 to watch Peterborough United. The average gate was 1,938.

Revamp at Granada

A REFIT costing thousands of pounds was carried out at the Granada cinema, St Peter's Hill. It took six men 360 hours to erect the scaffolding to paint the ceiling and another 240 hours to take it down. Five hundred square metres of carpet were laid in the circle and stalls.

Commercial TV OK

TELEVISION engineer John Birch, of Grantham Electrical Engineering, said commercial TV test pictures could be received in the borough with a modern set, a good aerial and a £5 adaptor.

Mountain bear makes his bid for freedom

A TWO metre tall, black Himalayan bear weighing 70kg, made a bid for freedom at Grantham Mid-Lent fair.

Two-year-old Teddy got stage fright before his debut at the sideshow Jungle Pit. He broke his chain lead and ran off along Wide Westgate.

Children and adults scattered in panic as the giant bear ran towards the railway bridge with trainer Johnny Hayes in pursuit.

Mr Hayes caught hold of the broken chain as Teddy reached Harlaxton Road. He calmed down the animal and escorted him back to his cage. Mr Hayes said afterwards: "I don't think Teddy was dangerous, he was just a little scared."

Power man puts town factories into a spin

CEMENT mixers ran backwards and drills spun anticlockwise as electricity supplies in town went haywire. Gonerby Hill Foot factories Fencraft Engineering and Vacu-Lug Traction Tyres found strange things happening when their machines were switched on.

They all went into reverse.

An East Midlands Electricity Board spokesman said: "An oversight by one of our engineers was the cause.

"A new installation was not carefully checked and unfortunately there were crossed leads."

Billy the hero save family from blaze

BLACK and white mongrel Billy, bought for only 10p out of sympathy from Grantham market a month earlier, saved five people from certain death.

Mr and Mrs E White and their three children, Raymond (4), Johnny (3) and Lorraine (18 months), were asleep at their Harrowby Hall estate cottage when Billy began a series of barks and howls.

Mr White went downstairs to investigate and found a cupboard in his living room ablaze.

He managed to douse the flames with water before the fire brigade arrived.

Praising Billy's actions, Deputy Chief Fire Officer J. Dixon said: "Had it not been for the little dog's alarm, the situation would have been serious.

"There was only one exit and the family would have been trapped."

Medics' radios waste of money says council

FITTING radios into Grantham's ambulances was too expensive, according to Kesteven County Council.

The proposed scheme which would have kept the vehicles in touch with their headquarters would have cost £42,000 a year.

The annual budget for the whole service was only £32,000.

Councillors said radio telephony would have "very limited value and a poor use of money."

Rugby plan is kicked into touch

RUGBY players were told housing is more important than sport.

Kesteven Rugby Club wanted to lease part of the Meres playing fields but town councillors ruled they could only rent it by the match like any other club. The Peacocks then asked for a three hectare plot of land in Earlesfield. The land was sufficient for a sports field, club-house and a small car park.

But the borough surveyor turned down their plea, saying 70 houses could be built on the land and homes had priority over sport.

Canberra crash

A CANBERRA reconnaissance aircraft crashed at Sudbrook, narrowly missing a farmhouse.

It exploded as it hit the ground, killing both pilot and navigator. Their bodies and engine parts were scattered over a 400m area.

Wing Cdr Robert Cole, 36, and Sqdn Ldr Peter Needham, 31, were based at West Raynham, Norfolk.

The plan crashed on W S Dean's farm and blazing fuel was scattered over a wide area, setting fire to a nearby copse. When the plane hit, crockery rattled on the tables of homes in the village.

Witnesses described seeing a mushroom-shaped cloud of black smoke hanging over the scene.

They were on a flight to Bovington, Herts, and may have been over Sudbrook to burn off fuel.

Holiday for seven in a taxi costing £25

SEVEN young men who went on a 16-day holiday in a taxi costing £25 arrived in Grantham after completing a European tour totalling 2,500 miles.

The 1936 Austin 12 carried all their luggage and camping equipment without a mishap.

Among them was Grantham man Peter Hall, son of Mr and Mrs Malcolm Hall, of the Drive.

Peter, 25, lived in Middlesbrough, his companions' native town.

The former King's School pupil, a foundry technician, and a former member of Kesteven RFC, said they bought the taxi two years before and this was their first outing.

Woman falls into pub cellar

THREE Newark men employed by Warwicks and Richardson brewery were each fined £1 after a woman fell into an unguarded cellar.

Mrs E Williams, of Grantley Cottages had been walking along Grantley Street when she fell in.

The cellar doors of the Golden Fleece had been left open by the three draymen and left unattended.

Mr Tinkler, mitigating, said it was not neglect but one of those things caused by a lack of attention and an unfortunate set of circumstances.

One over the eight

GRANTHAM FC went down to a record 9-1 defeat at Scarborough. The previous record reverse stood at 7-0, against Nottingham Forest in 1954 and Scarborough in 1951.

Dirt cheap

TOWN councillors increased the charges at Wharf Road slipper baths. In the first rise since 1951, the new charges were 1¾p higher at 7½p for a bath including use of towel and soap.

Riverside walk

GRANTHAM Council announced plans for a seven metre wide riverside walk from Witham Place to St Catherine's Road.

What a carve up

TOURISTS visiting St Wulfram's Church were slammed for cutting their initials into the ancient stonework.

Ecclesiastical architect Lawrence Bond said many initials had been scratched around the base of the spire and on the walls housing the tower staircase.

Mr Bond said: "If this outrageous behaviour continues the privilege of ascending the tower will have to be withdrawn."

Sawmill Fire

EMPLOYEES at Belvoir estates sawmill formed a bucket chain to put out a blaze which began in a creosoting shed. Their action prevented a more serious fire before the fire brigade arrived. The cost of damage was put at £250.

Slid into trouble

A 13-year-old boy had a lucky escape while sliding on the road in East Street. King's School pupil Francis O'Donnell suffered a fractured collarbone when he collided with a car driven by the head of a local painting firm John Coxworth. Children who previously prepared the 30m downhill slide helped remove it with salt.

Francis's brother Alistair (12) said: "The car skidded to a halt but Francis kept going". He hit the car headlamp with his shoulder. He was taken to hospital and released after treatment.

Window escape

DRIVER Sidney Bills and four passengers in his car escaped injured when it overturned at North Witham. They all escaped by crawling through a side window. The car was extensively damaged.

Duke to separate

THE Duke of Rutland (36) and his wife Anne announced they were to divorce. The couple married in April 1946 at St Margaret's, Westminster.

They had one daughter, Charlotte Louisa, born in 1947.

Petrol rationed

GRANTHAM Post Office was issuing petrol coupons for motorists, introduced because of the Suez crisis.

Cinema shuts

THE final curtain fell at the Picture House (pictured) on St Peter's Hill.

The cinema, the town's first purpose built one, was owned by the Campbell family until it was bought by the Granada Group.

Opened in 1916, the final performance was Reap the Wild Wind.

Grantham in the News 1957

Frankie goes to the hairdressers

CROWDS line High Street as heartthrob singer Frankie Vaughan drove into town.

He was there to promote Griffins hair salon, which had a visit from comedian Benny Hill in the same year.

Trainspotting hits the buffers at rail station

TRAINSPOTTERS were given the red card at Grantham railway station.

It followed complaints to British Railways that the schoolboys' paradise was becoming a nightmare for travellers.

Railway officials put their foot down when things came to a head during the summer holidays.

Many of young spotters arrived at the station from Nottingham and other stations to see the cream of the Eastern Region.

They were hoping to bring their Ian Allen log books up to date.

Magistrates supported the ban and fined three boys for trespassing.

They were sitting on the bridge over the pedestrian subway taking engine numbers.

But when a light engine came along, the youngsters had to swing their legs over to the other side of the parapet to let it pass safely.

Bell boy's record is a big hit in town

JOHNNY Rumfitt, a bellboy on the Queen Mary, decided to make a record while on a visit to New York.

He recorded Singing the Blues, which he sent to Granada cinema manager Harry Sanders with a message to play it for his friends on Sunday evening. And the audience on the Sunday night, when Mr San-ders showcased local talent, loved it.

The recording was on a Voice-o-Graph disc, without music.

According to his mum, Johnny, who later became known as Ricky Elvin, did not make the record on the spur of the moment.

She said: "He used to sit by the fire and tell me that one day he would join a ship's crew and bring back wonderful presents.

Before joining Cunard, the former pupil of Huntingtower Secondary School worked for grocers Parker & Co, of London Road.

Johnny said: "I'm working hard to become a commissioned waiter.

The circus comes to Grantham

SIR Robert Fossett's Circus came to town and the stars were the performing elephants. They arrived by train before marching along Station Road (pictured), Wharf Road and St Catherine's Road before turning towards Wyndham Park where the circus was held.

Town is bugged by Asian flu outbreak

ASIAN flu struck in Grantham, forcing hundreds of children to stay off school.

At one stage only a third of the pupils arrived for lessons.

Grantham Hospital was also hit. All wards were shut except for emergencies as staff were hit by the bug. As staff returned, others reported sick.

In September, doctors said it was getting worse with one surgery reporting 140 new victims a day. At first only children and teenagers fell ill but as time went on old people became vulnerable.

A quarter of the telephonists at the GPO exchange were off sick although postmen generally escaped the worst of it.

Seventeen railwaymen were hit by the bug on one day and the remaining staff went on to 12-hour shifts to cover.

Town loses its bearings

RANSOME and Marles Bearings closed its factory on Springfield Road, putting 80 out of work.

Other staff were transferred to the Newark factory.

Where there's a will

A WOMAN who bequeathed her Pyrenean Mountain dog to a friend, left her executors with a headache when the beneficiary refused it.

The giant dog, weighing 55kg, is costing the estate £1 a week in food bills while the lawyers sort it out.

The dog, Sylvanus de Montlouis was owned by the late Ethel Topham who left it to a friend. But her friend was unable to care for such a large animal.

It had hardly led a dog's life, travelling only in the cleanest taxis. Miss Topham had paid £21 for him but he won several awards at dog shows around the country.

Burglars bolted as sergeant slept

CHEEKY thieves stole into Bottesford police station while Sgt Edgar Wright, his wife and police cadet son were soundly asleep upstairs.

They entered through the front door and on seeing a bread bin in the hall, helped themselves to food.

It is believed they decided to flee on seeing the sergeant's tunic hanging on a peg.

They made off with a crash helmet and a pair of gauntlets, which were later discovered outside. outside.

Vagabonds look to the big time

MILLIONS of BBC TV viewers watched Grantham group the Vagabonds win £100 as runners up in the final of the National Skiffle Championships, at the Locarno ballroom, Streatham, London.

They were among more than 6,000 groups who entered the contest earlier in the year.

Judges included TV pop show Six-Five Special host Josephine Douglas and band leaders Ray Ellington and Oscar Rabin.

The group, featuring Roy Taylor (guitar), Brian Locking (bass), Roy Clark (guitar) and Mick Fretwell (drums) appeared at the legendary rock 'n' roll venue the Two I's coffee bar, Soho, the following night.

They were spotted by an agent who said they may well appear in a new Tommy Steele film.

During the evening, they were joined by singer Wee Willie Harris.

Two days later, the Vagabonds appeared at BMARCo's Hall in Grantham, in front of a huge local crowd.

Afterwards, Roy Taylor said: "It was like a dream. We hope we will not wake up too soon."

The group also got a three-appearance contract on BBC TV's Six-Five Special.

Joe gets a job

GRANTHAM MP Joseph Godber was appointed joint Parliamentary Secretary to the Ministry of Agriculture, Fisheries and Food by Prime Minister Harold Macmillan.

Plane crashes in field

A TWO-man crew and three passengers escaped unhurt when their twin-engine Anson overshot the runway at RAF Spitalgate.

It ploughed through a hedge, crossed the busy road unscathed and crashed into a field, ripping off the undercarriage and damaging the underside.

New home for bank

THE Westminster Bank's newly opened premises on St Peter's Hill were the most modern in the country.

It was built on the site of the former Cleveland Hotel.

Half jobless are men

UNEMPLOYMENT in Grantham stood at 289 in January.

There were 153 men, 110 women, eight boys and 18 girls out of work.

At Colsterworth, there were four men and eight women jobless.

Painting by Constables

POLICE bosses agreed to put aside £40 for tools for their constables to decorate their tied houses. The sets, including a paste board, a paste brush, a trestle table and scissors were kept at the police station for officers to borrow.

New finds at hotel

REDECORATING work at the Angel and Royal Hotel revealed interesting finds. A Tudor fireplace was discovered behind panelling in the drawing room to the left of the arch while a false ceiling was removed, exposing original oak beams.

Great news for hikers

A PAIR of semi-detached houses on Dudley Road were converted to a hostel by the Youth Hostel Association. The town council said it had no objection as far as the loss of housing accommodation was concerned.

Measles on the increase

THERE were 13 cases of whooping cough in January compared with only one the previous month according to the medical officer's report. Cases of measles in schools also leapt in the same period, from four to 32.

Rock 'n' roll is here to stay

ROCK 'n' Roll came to Grantham, where the very first session was staged at BMARCo social club, Springfield Road, in February.

While other clubs had notices saying "jiving and bopping prohibited" the cool cats at BMARCo were throwing their young chicks about in a jiving competition.

The music was supplied by the Vagabonds.

New school ceiling falls

THERE was an extended holiday for the 570 pupils at St Wulfram's School, Queensway, when the ceiling in the dining hall collapsed.

The school, opened only three months earlier, was shut for nearly three weeks while experts studied the cause.

Other schools using a similar building system were also shut as a precaution.

Card sharps at the castle

THREE men were each jailed for nine months after being caught cheating at cards at Belvoir Castle. They were taking part in the final of a whist drive. The men, two from Sheffield and one from Berkshire, pleaded not guilty at Leicester court. When one of them was found to have spare playing cards in his pocket, he said he was "shocked".

Edgar's weighty problem

GRANTHAM St John's forward Edgar Hanson missed his club's vital Lincoln League match against Saxilby.

Also a member of Grantham Physical Culture Club, he dropped a weight on his foot, leaving him in plaster. But he wasn't training. He was reaching for something on the shelf where the weight was stored, and it dropped on to his toes.

Catholics take to the streets

THE Corpus Christi procession of St Mary the Immaculate Church traditionally confined itself to the church. But this year, for the first time, it was decided to take it on to the streets, with a service in Wyndham Park. These children are part of the parade in Chapel Street.

Indoor pool

Grantham council's ruling Labour group said: "The desirability of covered swimming is beyond dispute.

"As soon as the financial and other difficulties become more favourable, practical steps will be taken to bring this into effect."

A spokesman said the pool would be convertible and also used for dancing, exhibitions, concerts and indoor sport.

Town on target

A YEAR-long appeal by Grantham FC to keep the club in the Midland League reached its £2,000 target.

It was backed by Flowers Brewery, of London Road.

Hart less

THE Hand & Hart, Wharf Road, and the Blue Dog, Watergate, were closed. Licences were transferred to Mowbray's Brewery for future use.

New reservoir

A FIVE million litre reservoir was opened on the corner of Gorse Lane and Kitty Briggs Lane, the biggest in the area.

It was lined by eight kilometres of wire, covered in mortar.

Duchess is fined

KATHLEEN, Duchess of Rutland, mother to the Duke, was fined £4 for obstruction and £2 for driving without a licence.

Pc Dachtler said she was parked diagonally between two cars outside the George Hotel.

Admitting her licence had expired, she said it was usually renewed by her chauffeur.

High Street development plans are unveiled

HIGH Street shops (pictured) were awaiting demolition to make way for the new F W Woolworth store.

The frontage of the Grantham Journal was also set to be demolished, to be incorporated in the new building.

The newspaper had been on the site since taking over the Mail Hotel in 1868.

The stone-built Horse and Jockey was to be pulled down for a new branch of Fine Fare.

The White Hart was not affected by the scheme

Woolworth's would move from the Market Place.

Further developments were also being planned on the other side of High Street, including the Red Lion.

Grantham in the News 1958

Roy eager but the Vagabonds split

GRANTHAM rock 'n' roll sensation Roy Taylor signed a 54-month contract with agents Larry Parnes and John Kennedy – who also had Tommy Steele on their books – in April. The deal included TV appearances and tours of South Africa and Europe.

Roy, 17, was to be re-launched as Vince Eager. The contract was worth £3,000 pa of which the singer got 60 per cent.

His debut, with local group The Vagabonds, was at Southsea, standing in for top-of-the-bill Marty Wilde who had a throat infection.

But by July it went sour. Although Vince continued in show business, the Vagabonds broke up disenchanted. Roy Clark left for his National Service and Brian Locking teamed up with singer Terry Dene.

Drummer Mick Fretwell said: "We were living on promises. We had six jobs. We earned £10 on the first night and £20 for the other five.

"I left Grantham with a substantial bank balance.

"Now all I have in the world is £1.25

"I'm hoping to renew my apprenticeship at Ruston and Hornsby's."

Six-year-old boy was sitting on petrol tank

A MOTORCYCLIST was fined £1 for driving while having a six-year-old boy sitting astride the petrol tank.

Police stopped them as they rode along Belvoir Road, Bottesford.

Belvoir magistrates were told the rider stopped at the police request and the boy almost fell to the ground. The Redmile biker told the bench he was taking the boy for a haircut and believed it was safer to sit in front of him than on a seat behind.

He said: "I usually use a sidecar but I borrowed this bike.

Players in crash

FOOTBALLERS Aubrey Southwell (36), and Eric Lister, both with Boston United, were injured when their car collided with a lorry on Barrowby Hill. Both received head injuries.

A Boys' Central School old boy, Mr Southwell was a previous captain of Notts County.

Where's my stockings?

A PILLION passenger on a motorcycle travelling through Morton saw her nylon stockings disintegrate after being splashed by a chemical.

The chemical, sulphuric hydroxide, had leaked from a tanker, leaving a trail through the village.

The woman was unharmed, although villagers had to tolerate an obnoxious smell during their Sunday dinner.

Only woman councillor

SECRETARY of Grantham Labour Party Elsie Davies, became the borough council's only woman member. She was returned unopposed for St John's ward.

Motorist hits policeman

A TRAVELLER from London got a shock when he opened his car door in Church Street, Grantham.

It was struck by a bobby on a bicycle. Pc Dachtler was unhurt, but he charged the motorist with interrupting the free passage of the road.

The motorist was fined £2.

Coal lorry plunges into coal merchant's home

A LORRY carrying 12 tonnes of coal careered down Barrowby Hill when its brakers failed.

The truck, which came from Nottingham, crossed the Great North Road into Broad Street, past Little Gonerby School – uprooting a tree on the way – and into the front of 6 Albion Place.

It was the home of retired coal merchant J W Storey (82).

The garden wall was smashed, the lorry's front wheels were broken off and the cab severely damaged.

The load went through the window, filling the living room.

The driver, Bernard Gallagher, of Nottingham, was miraculously uninjured, the only casualty being Mr Storey's granddaughter Julie (16) who received a cut on her chin.

J A C Cooper, sales manager of Witham Garage, Barrowby Road, said the driver was sounding the horn all along.

He said: "He deserves a medal for this.

"Because of his actions, other motorists, especially at crossroads, managed to avoid his lorry."

Teenagers can marry

A YOUNG couple living in Grantham were given consent to marry by Spittlegate magistrates.

The 16-year-old girl said they had planned to marry the previous week, but her mother had withdrawn her consent.

The 19-year-old groom, who earned £6.82 working in a butcher's shop, said they wanted a house as they had enough furniture already.

Probation officer Miss Broadhead said the girl was expecting a baby but her mother still couldn't make up her mind.

TV star opens TV show

TV personality MacDonald Hobley arrived at the Westgate Hall in September 1958 to open Westmoreland's TV & Radio exhibition. Behind him are John Barber's shop for the decorator and Sharpes seed merchants, a forerunner of garden centres.

More are going overseas for their summer holidays

PEOPLE in Grantham were beginning to say goodbye to Skegness and Cleethorpes for their annual break.

Instead they were looking overseas for summer holidays.

Grantham Travel Agency said Austria and Spain were the favourite destinations.

Both cost £25 for 15 days while five days in Belgium cost £9.85.

But winter holidays got the cold shoulder.

One or two people were skiing but there were no takers for sun-seeking holidays at Christmas.

Air force demolishes old cottages for guardroom

A ROW of century-old cottages which stood on Somerby Hill was demolished.

Spittlegate Cottages were pulled down to make way for a new guardroom for RAF Spitalgate.

Doctor's death

DR CHARLES Frier, died at his Barrowby Road home. He was 87. Dr Frier began practising in Grantham in 1896. A magistrate, he also set up a fund to send crippled children to the seaside each year.

It's back to school

BOYS and girls had to return to school because of a lack of jobs. At the end of the summer term, 87 boys and 49 girls had failed to find employment. The total unemployment for the town in September stood at 363, excluding 180 workers on short time claiming benefit.

Light work

JOSEPH Wright, of 44 London Road, spent two weeks marooned at the Wolf Rock lighthouse, off Land's End. The Ruston and Hornsby engineer, who was there to test engines, was stranded by gales sweeping in from the Atlantic ocean.

Puffed out

GRANTHAM witnessed the first signs of the end of the age of steam, when the Talisman train sped through town hauled for the first time by a diesel-electric locomotive.

Scouts build on success

BOY scouts of the 7th Grantham (St Johns) pack built their own club house in Earlesfield Lane.

They toiled with the help of volunteer builders to replace their wooden hut.

The venture cost £3,000.

Dangerous criminals helped themselves while family slept

TWO escaped prisoners from Rampton Mental Institution, broke into a Grantham home and helped themselves to food while a family slept. Police were hunting for them in the area after finding a Morris Oxford car they had stolen in Yorkshire, at Spittlegate Level. After stealing cash from a handbag in the car, they broke into St Wulfram's School to lay low.

Later that night, they felt hungry and broke into the Queensway home of Mr and Mrs Stan Dugdale and their children Roberta (3) and Michael (16 months).

After leaving, they stole a coal lorry belonging to Parsons Bros and Snape, from Melbourne Road.

The Dugdales discovered the break-in when they woke up the following morning.

The men had left a note saying: "Sorry but we're hungry. We wish you a Merry Christmas."

Mrs Dugdale said they ate one of the children's chocolate mice. They took her husband's mackintosh – which was recovered when the men were recaptured – but left her purse untouched.

As the Dugdales were going away for Christmas, the escapees had to settle for a diet of bananas, biscuits, cakes and a jar of mincemeat.

Aveling-Barford in major export drive

AVELING Barford won a major order for dumper trucks and other road making plant from Argentina.

The order was so big, a special train had to be booked to take the machinery, destined for Buenos Aires, to the docks. The driver is pictured (above) checking the lamps as Aveling Barford bosses join railway staff to watch it leave from the company's sidings at Grantham.

Foundry shuts

RUSTON and Hornsby closed its foundry in Spring Gardens.

The work was transferred to Lincoln, leaving the Grantham building to be used for storage.

Ninety jobs were affected.

Head says goodbye

HEADMASTER of Grantham King's School, for 19 years, W J Huggins (59) retired.

He joined the school shortly before the outbreak of war.

End of road for tractors

TRACTOR makers Newman Industries shut down its Springfield Road factory, shedding 100 jobs. Employees were offered alternative work at Yate, Gloucestershire.

A company spokesman blamed a lack of skilled labour in the Grantham area.

Ex-vicar dies

CANON Harold Leeke (70) died just four months after retiring as Vicar of St Wulfram's.

He was buried at Marlow and a requiem mass was held in Grantham.

1959 Grantham in the News

HILL & CO.

(Grantham) LTD.
20 MARKET PLACE, GRANTHAM
Phone 501

INTRODUCE
Brides, Bridesmaids'
and Cocktail Dresses

All Types
Headdresses and
veils

BRIDES' GOWNS
from £8/8/- to £19

Skillington makes Clear Profit

SKILLINGTON trained Clear Profit was one of only eight horses to complete the Grand National.
It came third behind Merryman II and Badanloch.

Trainer R L Newton had a half share in the horse until a week before the race. Most Skillington villagers had a flutter on the horse and were well rewarded. It came home at 20-1, returning £6 for every £1 each way bet.

Cliff edges the hearts of locals

CROWDS of screaming teenage girls thronged the stage door at the Granada cinema, hoping for a glimpse of their hero.

They were waiting to see 18-year-old rock 'n' roll sensation Cliff Richard who had just topped the bill with his group The Drifters in the show Let's Move It.

The host of TV's Oh Boy had given an electrifying performance and was greeted by screams from hysterical girl fans. Earlier in the afternoon he went shopping for a black shirt, but failed to find one. He was also besieged by autograph hunters when he went to White and Sentance, St Peter's Hill, to buy records. Even before he arrived, local girls were souvenir hunting. No sooner did cinema staff put up the posters than lovesick girls were taking them away. Also on the bill were Wee Willie Harris, Johnny Duncan and his Blue Grass Boys, the Bachelors and a young comedian, Jimmy Tarbuck.

Preservation of time

THE Guildhall clock, which had not been keeping good time, was restored.

Joe Harris and Jack Parker carried out the work, at a time when St Peter's Hill east was still open to traffic and signals were unnecessary.

New flats built by modern methods

FLATS built by the borough council on Grange Gardens, off Union Street, were nearing completion. They provided homes for 27 families at a cost of £37,000 using new Unity pre-cast methods.

Uncle Harry's back

'UNCLE' Harry Sanders returned to manage the Granada cinema. He left two years previously to run one at Kingston-on-Thames.

Jobless fall

UNEMPLOYMENT in Grantham fell from 310 in March to 265 in April. There were 107 men looking for work, 12 boys, 131 women and 14 girls.

Boarding fees hike

FEES for boarders at Grantham King's School rocketed from £130 to £150 per term.

The increase by Kesteven County Council followed a £907 deficit on last year's accounts.

Car park unready

THE new St Catherine's Road car park remained shut.

Filling material had not properly consolidated and more material was need to finish the work.

Tender accepted

FOUR tenders were received for five flats and a shop at the junction of Harrowby Lane and Edinburgh Road.

The lowest for £8,615 from A. Richmond and Sons of Retford was accepted.

Too noisy

RESIDENTS in the west of town were putting together a petition demanding the closure of BMARCo's test firing range.

Gasworks demolished

THE canalside, Victorian buildings of Grantham Gasworks were demolished as town gas and coke were no longer produced there.

The gasometers remained for storage only until North Sea Gas was discovered.

Small pox is finished for good says medical officer

SMALL pox was a thing of the past, medical officer Dr J H C Clarke told the county council.

He said there had been no recorded cases in town since 1931.

And for the eighth successive year, there had been no diphtheria reported.

But there were 2,217 cases of measles, 156 whooping cough, 82 scarlet fever and 16 erysipelas. Poliomyelitis was down to three cases compared with 30 the previous year.

Mayor goes underground

MAYOR Ernest Smith used to turn up in the most unlikely places.

Pictured above he is under Park Road with borough engineers inspecting the culvert which took the Mowbeck under Brook Street until it discharged in the River Witham near the White Bridge in Wyndham Park.

Farmers say kids should go nesting

MEMBERS of the Grantham NFU branch said children should be allowed to help them in their attack on the pigeon menace

A N Ballard, of Allington said: "Why not give children 2.5p an egg?

"The money could be given by Government instead of issuing cheap cartridges to farmers."

Airmen in a spin bale out to safety

TWO men, a pupil and his instructor, baled out to safety from their RAF Provost trainer when the plane broke into an uncontrollable spin at 7,000ft over Londonthorpe. They landed in a ploughed field, just missing telephone wires.

They were picked up near the High Dyke a few hundred metres from the wreckage by a passing motorist. They were unhurt.

The plane caused a two-metre crater in a wheatfield on the corner of Londonthorpe Lane, belonging to farmer Jack Lynn. Eye-witness Agnes Bland said: "I took no notice of it at first. It thought it was a jet.

"Then I saw the parachutes floating down and heard the crash."

There was no blaze although the plane broke into thousands of pieces.

Cinema for sale

SIGNS showing the Picture House was up for sale went up on the former cinema.

The St Peter's Hill building was owned by the Granada Group.

No rail closure

BRITISH Railways denied it planned to close the Grantham locomotive depot.

It said the 300 jobs in the motive power department were safe.

Johns go out of Cup

AN own goal by right-half Leverett 12 minutes from time, put Grantham St John's out of the FA Amateur Cup.

They went out at Harrowby Fields by 2-1 to Aspley Old Boys.

New school plea

THREE hundred parents of Girls' Central School pupils unanimously backed plans to build a new school off Harlaxton Road.

But they said it must remain a girls-only school with a separate one for boys built elsewhere.

Supermac backs Honest Joe

PRIME Minister Harold Macmillan visited Grantham to support the Conservative candidate Joe Godber. He was accompanied by his wife Lady Dorothy.

Mr Godber was returned in October's General Election with an increased majority.

He polled 27,482 votes against Labour's Thomas Skeffington Lodge's 20,867 in a straight fight.

Godber's majority in 1955 was 2,375. On his return, he kept his post as Parliamentary Secretary to the Ministry of Agriculture.

Skeleton discovered

A GRANTHAM man was ordered to stop digging his garden after he came across human bones. Mr A S Brown, of 84 Belton Lane, came across the skeleton while digging a hole to bury feathers.

An examination by Dr J H Hopper revealed it to be about 150 years old.

New home for police

POLICE moved to their new headquarters at Stonebridge House, St Catherine's Road. It put the town force under the same roof for the first time since 1947. Up to then, officers had been either at the town office bus station, or the court house, London Road.

Arthur dies

FORMER Mayor Arthur Eatch died aged 82. Up until two years before he was still active with the building firm he began 55 years earlier.

Rolled over

NO one was hurt in this collision between a Rover and a Riley Elf, although the latter was knocked over on to his side.

It happened on the corner of Avenue Road and Welham Street, in front of Pidcock's maltings. But it did prove to be a big attraction, especially for the inquisitive young boys in the area.

Unlucky breaks for Grantham schoolgirl

MARGARET Carr (13) had more than her share of unlucky breaks. She spent her summer holidays with a leg in plaster after falling off a wall.

The St Mary's School pupil had already badly sprained her ankle at the Mid-Lent Fair. Shortly after the cast was removed, she climbed a Wyndham Park tree, fell seven metres, and broke both wrists. Former home guard Mr C Coulson, who was passing, applied first aid before calling an ambulance.

Pub shuts after over a century

THE Marquis of Granby pub, Barrowby, called time after more than a century.

A spokesman for owner Flowers Brewery said it was losing money and some nights there was only one customer in the bar room.

It left the White Swan and the British Legion club to cater for the village's 700 population.

The last landlady was Sylvia Payne, whose great-grandmother took over in the 1880s and began a dynasty of women licensees.

Dear stay

IT cost £24.10 a week to keep a patient in Grantham Hospital, according to the NHS, compared with £29.65 at Newark.

Royal Buckminster

BUCKMINSTER'S water tower played an important part in the Queen's Christmas broadcast. BBC Technicians spent their Christmas with a mast linking Sandringham with the rest of the country.

Not the right spirit

THE introduction of a Christmas tree outside St Wulfram's Church was marred when thieves made off with the lights.

New name

THE stretch of Avenue Road between Welham Street and Sandon Road was renamed Stonebridge Road.

Police houses at the top of the hill were renumbered.

Band hit by apathy

A FUND-raising fete by Grantham Pimpernels hit a sour note when only 100 people turned up. The carnival band marched through town to the field on New Beacon Road, where the garden fete was held. Overall, the band made £15.

1960 Grantham in the News

All rev'd up

CLERGYMEN and Church-wardens went on the march to draw attention to the Methodist Mission in the town.

They were led by the Rev A J Bowerts of Bridge End Road Wesleyan Church. They are photographed outside gentlemen's outfitters George Mills, High Street.

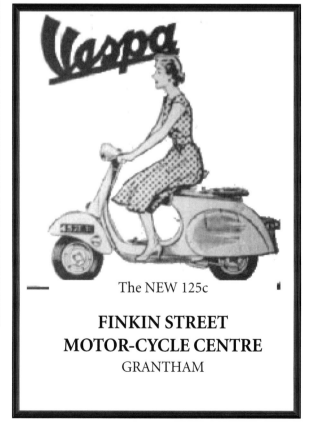
Population up

THE population of Grantham stood at 24,480, according to the Registrar General's annual estimate.

Sleaford was 7,440 and Boston 24,230.

Witham at flood level

HEAVY rains caused flooding around the county.

The Witham flowing through Wyndham Park was five feet deep in places.

The cavern under the van is the culvert discharging the Mowbeck into the principal river.

The girls take over at RAF Spitalgate

GRANTHAM saw an influx of uniformed women as RAF Spitalgate was taken over by the Women's Royal Air Force.

After a skeleton staff had run the station for just over a year, a fleet of coaches delivered 350 girls and NCOs from their former base, RAF Wilmslow, near Manchester.

RAF Spitalgate became the only WRAF depot in the United Kingdom. Girls aged 17 and over completed six weeks basic training there before moving on to specialist trade training schools.

The barrack blocks were redecorated in modern pastel shades, mainly mushroom, with flowered curtains hanging from pelmet rails.

The influx was well received by the town's publicans and even more especially its young men.

No one way

PLANS to turn Rycroft Street into a one-way system were turned down by the borough council.

Electrifying job

A WAGES clerk was required by East Midlands Electricity Board.

Salary began at £330pa for an 18-year-old rising to a maximum of £640pa.

A job as junior assistant at the public library, with at least five O levels, paid £240-£595pa.

Going pear-shaped

A PEAR-shaped traffic island was installed at the Harrowby Lane junction with New Beacon Road at the cost of £230.

No to the verge

A REQUEST by residents of Belton Lane to allow them to park their cars on the grass verges in front of their homes, was dismissed outright by the town's highways committee.

No time for old timers

ARMS maker BMARCo announced it would no longer employ workers who were aged 65 or over.

About a dozen men were dismissed with a week's notice, five of them receiving a pension.

Top US star in town

AN excited teenager leaped on to the Granada stage as top US singer Gene Vincent was performing. She was escorted back to the main floor by a member of staff. An enthusiastic audience clapped, stamped and whistled throughout as he built up to his climax, his big hit, Be-bop-a-lula.

New rinks

TAILOR Colin Tipler rolled the first wood for the official opening of Bjorlow's Bowling Club on Earlesfield Lane.

No cribbing

FOUNDER and secretary of Grantham and District Cribbage League Bill Bryan attained his ambition.

As predicted, he retired on his 80th birthday after being in the job for nine years. He was succeeded by Pat Andrew.

One player remarked: "I wonder if Pat will last as long as Bill did?"

Singer in accident

SUPERSTAR Shirley Bassey, 23, was only slightly hurt when her Rolls Royce collided with a van in a 65mph crash and ended up on its roof on the A1 south of Grantham. She was freed by Wally Layne of Great Gonerby.

Countess battles blaze to save her stately home

THE Countess of Ancaster mobilised estate workers in rescue operations when fire broke out at Grimsthorpe Castle. Ignoring falling debris and getting drenched by firemen's hoses, she guided firemen through the labyrinth of rooms to the seat of the fire.

And when the library upstairs became threatened, she was part of a human chain delivering the books to safety. The fire began in a linen room on the top storey of the building which dates from the 13th Century. It then raced through a false roof.

Firemen had to break down locked doors and pull down ceilings to get at the blaze.

They were impeded by molten lead dripping from the roof. Water had to be pumped from a lake a kilometre away.

But the timely action was worth the effort and the castle was able to be restored.

Royal link with pub

THE Royal Queen, the pub which opened in Belton Lane in April, was named by Lady Desiree Welby, wife of the chairman of Holes Brewery.

The name surprised most Granthamians, who wrongly believed it referred to Queen Victoria.

A former professional singer, Lady Desiree recalled singing Six Dukes went Fishing, a song which referred to the Royal Queen of Grantham. The queen in the song was Margaret of Anjou, who married Henry VI in 1445. Grantham was part of her dowry.

The pub had no cellar. Instead it had a cork-lined refrigerated room.

Mine hosts were Bill and Joyce Pickin, formerly of the Thorold Arms, Marston.

Farm fire at Pointon

HOUSEWIVES in a row of cottages at Pointon had to leave their homes as they put up their Christmas decorations, when fire swept through a neighbouring farm. Firemen helped remove furniture as a wood mill at Pointon House Farm – where explosive materials were stored – went up in flames.

Employees were away at the time, acting as beaters on a shoot.

MP promoted

GRANTHAM MP Joe Godber was appointed Parliamentary Under-Secretary at the Foreign Office.

The post carried a salary of £3,250 a year.

Murder Miles

RENEWED demands for a Grantham bypass came after more deaths on Spittlegate Level.

Known as Murder Miles, the stretch between Little Ponton and Saltersford became the most notorious on the A1 trunk road. Up to 20 road deaths a year on the mile long stretch were not uncommon.

Smoke killed brave officer

A FORMER Army officer with a distinguished First World War record, died in Newark Hospital.

General Sir George de Symons Barrow (95), of Long Bennington was admitted a month earlier after his lighted pipe set fire to his clothes. He was burned on the thigh and right arm.

Recording accidental death, coroner J B Norman told an inquest: "It was unfortunate that such a distinguished career should come to an end by such a simple accident."

He was mentioned in dispatches eight times.

Workmen buried as trench collapsed

TWO pipelayers were completed buried when the walls of a five-metre trench they were working in collapsed. Fellow workmen dug furiously to free them, getting their heads above the soil in seconds.

It was a further seven minutes before they were finally released.

Arthur Randall (36), of Folkingham, received a bruised left shoulder and Peter Shearing, from Nottingham, had a bruised right hip.

Both were sent home after a check-up at Grantham Hospital.

The men, employees of Wimpey, were laying a storm drain in Earlesfield Lane, close to the Grantham Canal.

The walls were shored by timber but it could not prevent the collapse of clay with overlay sand.

There was no warning. Site manager Mike Berry said the two men were lucky to be alive. Wimpey was widening Earlesfield Lane and laying sewers for the new Earlesfield housing estate being built on the opposite bank.

Shopped for service

THREE shopkeepers were each fined £1 for selling non-perishable goods after 1pm on a Wednesday.

Frank Bush, of Dudley Road, and Raymond Finch, of Granville Street, were both seen selling packets of detergent and John Baker, of New Beacon Road, a packet of sugar. It was the first prosecution since early closing moved from Thursday to Wednesday.

Smokeless zone

THE area north of Harrowby Lane became a smokeless zone, but over 300 residents wanted it scrapped.

George Foster, of the Grantham Coal Merchants Association, said the scheme was a farce. He said: "This is not a black area at all – it's very nearly the countryside."

Plucking for opera

FORMER Boys' Central School pupil David Snell accepted an invitation to join the Covent Garden Opera House orchestra. The 23-year-old harpist was also pianist in Jimmy Carr's dance band. He learned to play the harp under Marie Goossens (of Mrs Dale's Diary fame) while on national service with the Royal Artillery.

Heifer goes on the rampage

AN Aberdeen Angus heifer weighing 400kg, prolonged its life by two hours, when it escaped from the Inner Street slaughterhouse dragging 16m of chain.

Pedestrians were forced to leap out of the way as it darted through the town pursued by slaughterer Ted Everton. It raced to the junction of Bridge End Road and London Road, then back towards the town, the trailing chain ripping the wings from parked cars.

One man was dragged from his feet as he tried to grab the chain.

More cars were damaged as the beast rampaged down Oxford Street and up College Street.

It was finally brought under control on High Street by a drayman making deliveries to a pub.

He managed to grasp the chain and secure it to his lorry.

There was no reprieve for the brave beast. It was taken back to the slaughterhouse and destroyed.

Brick shortage

HOUSE prices could go up by as much as £40 because of the brick shortage. The rural council said bungalows at Pickworth, Sudbrook, Colsterworth, Great Gonerby and Old Somerby were under threat.

Michael Syddall, of merchants Arthur Syddall & Co said the situation was worse than just after the war.

He said: "There is a production bottle neck and the kilns just aren't turning them out."

Rock star Vince quits home town show

GRANTHAM-born TV and stage pop-star Vince Eager pulled out of the show due to visit his home town.

He was furious that his spot in the 10-week touring show, Idols on Parade, had been slashed from 30 minutes to 12.

Vince – real name Roy Taylor – was due to appear at the Granada with 14 other recording stars.

He said: "It means a personal loss of £3,000 but it's a matter of prestige. They invited me to take part and I was thrilled to be playing in my home town.

"The organisers said I would have 30 minutes, putting on a similar act to the summer season I did at Great Yarmouth.

"Then they told me I would have only 12 minutes. I can't do my act in that time."

But Vince was determined to play in town at a later date.

He said: "I've been looking forward to playing Grantham for a long time and I'm sorry it folded up like this at the last minute." He told the Granada Group he would play at the theatre at a future date with his fee going to the town's Handicapped Children's Association.

Farmer escapes bull attack

A BOTTESFORD farmer had a miraculous escape when attacked by a Friesian bull.

John Goodson, 23, of Belvoir Road, saved his life after ripping the ring from the animal's nose. As the bull writhed in pain, John scrambled clear.

Farm worker John Hodson drove a Land Rover into the field to help his employer.

The beast attacked the vehicle with such ferocity, Mr Hodson had to abandon the attempt.

An Army marksman killed it with one shot.

Castle homes

THE Ministry of Housing overruled Kesteven County Council's objections and allowed 10 bungalows to be built on the site of Folkingham Castle. The inspector said as there was little chance of the keep and medieval remains being tidied up. He said the site may as well be made useful.

Blaze rips through paper warehouse

HUGE flames were seen for miles around as they engulfed John Lee's warehouse, London Road, causing £50,000 damage.

Hundreds of tonnes of stock were destroyed and only a charred shell of the building remained.

The alarm was raised at 9pm on a Saturday and eight fire crews were soon on the scene. A fire brigade spokesman said: "The flames spread at a running pace. They leapt past our water barrage."

The heat was so intense it caused the main wall to bulge and sway, putting firemen in constant danger.

The asbestos roofing exploded, sending long tongue-like flames high into the clear night sky.

Fanned by strong breezes, the hot embers threatened neighbouring buildings and residents were ready for immediate evacuation.

The main road was blocked for hours by fire engines and thousands of spectators, returning from the pubs and dance halls. Firefighters risked their lives on the upper storey, yet amazingly the only injury was a twisted ankle.

Even more incredible was that the blaze stopped less than a metre from a tank containing 10,000 litres of petrol. A tank of paraffin also survived. The building was formerly Hornsby's blacksmiths shop.

Ninety per cent of the stock was destroyed although the lorries were driven to safety.

1961 Grantham in the News

Court swings in rockers' favour

ROCK 'n' rollers were allowed to continue to enjoy their favourite music at the Westgate Hall.

At a four-and-a-half minute hearing, the crowded licensing justices court was told that Grantham teenagers could continue to jive the night away.

The Town Clerk had received a letter from the George Hotel, calling for a halt to the bopping. It complained that the sound of beat groups was upsetting the hotel's guests.

The hotel owner demanded the dance organisers should either turn down the volume or be banned from the Westgate Hall. More than 400 angry teenagers, led by town councillors, took to the streets before the hearing in protest at the hotel's demands. Carrying placards such as "Get with it, George" and "Let's think about living" they held a silent vigil.

Parliament promotions

TWO MPs with Grantham connections were promoted.

Margaret Thatcher, member for Finchley, was appointed Joint Parliamentary Secretary at the Ministry of Pensions and National Insurance. The new position, which carried a £3,250 a year salary, came as a birthday present for the former KGGS head girl. Also promoted was town MP Joe Godber. He moved from joint Under-Secretary to the Minister of State at the Foreign Office. He succeeded David Ormsby-Gore.

Rigid river

THE River Witham froze over for the first time in 60 years.

Many youngsters enjoyed the big freeze during the Christmas holidays, with tobogganing in the streets and skating on the frozen river and canal.

Rail aid for road

BRITISH Railways adapted a Great Ponton siding to aid the delivery of bulk cement for Grantham's £2 million A1 bypass. About 20,000 tonnes of cement was used at the rate of 600 tonnes a week.

Home start

BUNGALOWS and three-bedroomed semi-detached homes built on Dysart Road by H C Janes of Leicester, went on sale at £2,025 each.

The company's three-bedroomed detached homes, each with a garage, built on Harlaxton Road cost £2,625.

Front doors back

FRONT doors of eight council houses on Ermine Street, Ancaster, were restored at a cost of £100. They had been replaced, without the consent of tenants, as part of an improvement package. They were put back following intervention by local MP Joe Godber.

Housing shortage holds back industrial boom

GRANTHAM companies were being held back due to a lack of housing, town councillors were told.

Expansion was stunted by a shortage of skilled labour and accommodation, as the town to keep pace with its biggest industrial development.

The population was projected to swell from 25,000 to more than 40,000 in a short time.

Aveling Barford said it could set on a further 200 men immediately and Ruston and Hornsby wanted to divert work from its other factories.

Aveling Barford chairman Edward Barford said the company was losing orders because it could not turn out products fast enough.

Announcing profits of £728,000, managing director H C Ryan said: "We need 1,000 men for our planned expansion."

At BMARCo, general manager S C Lambert said: "We could start 200 skilled men immediately. Our expansion plans are held up by the lack of labour."

He said a company representative had been to Canada and reported 450 skilled engineers were willing to come to Grantham – if there was somewhere to live.

A plan to build 50 homes for employees on the company's Harlaxton Road sports ground was rejected by the town council.

Borough surveyor Jack Dean said 60 per cent of Grantham's products were exported.

He said: "My council is prepared to build 500 houses within 15 months to cater for industrial expansion." He said these would be built mostly at Allington, Harlaxton and Barrowby.

Plenty for Christmas

PEOPLE of Grantham were looking forward to Christmas as food became plentiful. Meat and plucked poultry hung from overhead rails showed a merry Christmas was inevitable. This picture was taken at Hammonds, Wharf Road.

Housing shocker for Harlaxton villagers

HARLAXTON residents were seething after hearing there were planning applications for more than 800 homes for the village.

The parish council wrote to the Minister of Housing saying as Harlaxton was the prettiest village around Grantham, it should be left alone.

Chairman K St J Mirrelees said:

"Nothing we can do will stop normal building expansion but we can ensure this is carried out carefully.

"The alternative, a purely commercial estate development, would mean the ruin of our village as we know it."

The county education committee agreed for the village to have a new school costing £11,900.

Shedding light on Cup

GRANTHAM Football Club reached the FA Cup first round for the first time in 12 years.

West Midlands hosts Brierley Hill allowed the visitors 80 of the best stand seats at 17½p each.

Standing was unlimited at 10p.

But Grantham bosses were unhappy with a proposed 3pm kick-off.

This meant playing much of the game under floodlights,

A town director said: "It would be a great advantage for them to play the second half under lights. "We aren't used to it."

Crossing keeper killed by train

A RAILWAY crossing keeper at Claypole was killed when he was struck by a goods train as he open the gates for a motorbike.

Johannes Rynenberg had just opened the Auster Fen gates. when it happened.

The motorcycle was written off but both rider and pillion passenger were unhurt.

Golden blood

THE Bishop of Grantham, the Rt Rev Anthonyn Otter, was the first person in Kesteven to be awarded with the gold award for giving 50 donations of blood.

In store

THE final act was played out for the Picture House, on St Peter's Hill. The last performance, had been Reap the Wild Wind, in 1956.

It was demolished to make way for Tesco's supermarket, the biggest grocery store in town. Nearby, the Horse and Jockey pub was demolished to make way for a branch of Boots.

Dear call

A NORFOLK lorry driver who used steel washers in a pay phone to call his wife was fined £15 by Grantham Magistrates.

He admitted making a total of seven phone calls from both Grantham and Long Bennington.

Coroner kept busy

GRANTHAM coroner John Pert had his busiest year ever, with 74 inquests.

Fifteen were deaths on the Murder Mile, Spittlegate Level.

Hospital scheme opens

THREE wards, the new nurses' home, a boiler house and engineer's department were opened at Grantham Hospital by Dr G E Godber of the Ministry of Health. Heb was brother of Grantham's MP Joseph Godber

The Minister said the £196,000 development ensured the future of the hospital.

Police cars worn out

POLICE cars are worn out at 100,000 miles, according to Lincolnshire's assistant chief constable A Johnson.

He said that was achieved in two years.

Turkeys destroyed

A FLOCK of turkeys, 15,000 of them, were destroyed because of fowl pest.

They were at Belvoir Turkey Farms, Belvoir.

Lambs to the slaughter

GRANTHAM and District Butchers' Association gave boy scouts and girl guides 250 lamb chops for their barbecue which was held on St Wulfram's vicarage lawn.

Seat of learning

A CLAIM that Grantham was the ideal site for the proposed Lincolnshire University was put before the county education committee.

Coun Stanley Foster said: "We gather a move in Cambridge favours Stamford for a satellite college because of the town's historic background.

"We must ensure the university is sited in its proper place, here in Grantham"

Canal closure

BRITISH Waterways said it planned to close the 33-mile long Grantham Canal, last used in 1936.

Anglers were up in arms at the plans and Bjorlow's tannery said it would have to close if its water supply was taken.

Bishop moves for railway

BISHOP of Lincoln, the Rt Rev Kenneth Riches, admitted to being a railway fan and asked to see the loco workshops and marshalling yards off Springfield Road. They were under threat of modernisation.

His wish was granted and officials took him and fellow clergy on a tour.

Kids help with circus

CHIPPERFIELD'S Circus came to town in November 1961, much to the delight of many a small boy who turned out to help set it up in Wyndham Park. In the background is the Boys' Central School.

No arms for pub

FLOWERS Brewery decided to change the name of the Railway Tavern, next door to the Granada cinema on St Peter's Hill.

The brewers renamed it the Guildhall Tavern although town councillors refused to give them permission to use the town's coat of arms on the inn sign.

Everest conqueror at school

SIR John Hunt who led the successful expedition to conquer Mt Everest in 1953 was in town.

He visited the Boys' Central School, Hill Avenue, to present boys with their Duke of Edinburgh awards.

He was secretary of the awards scheme.

He is pictured above walking up the 'Quad' as it was known, much to the delight of pupils.

War dead to move

GERMAN war dead were exhumed in Grantham and Londonthorpe cemeteries and transferred to a central one in Staffordshire.

Eight victims of the Second World War were removed from Grantham, three from a plane crash and five PoWs who died at Allington camp. Both Londonthorpe bodies were from the First World War.

Harbour blues

PLANS to turn the former Blue Harbour pub, Old Somerby, into a roadside cafe, were turned down by the county council.

They gave poor visibility and large numbers of vehicles as the reason.

New Inn

FLOWERS Brewery opened its newest pub at the Harlaxton Road and Springfield Road junction.

It was named the Sir Isaac Newton and Bill Bendall was appointed its first manager.

1962 Grantham in the News

Women refuse to move for new village bypass

WORK on the £10,000 Caythorpe bypass came to a halt when two women refused to leave their home which was in the way.

Mary Anne Scott (87) and her daughter Elsie May (60) lived in the house which prevented contractors from linking it up with the Grantham-Lincoln road leaving the bypass just 40 metres short.

They had been offered a council house but Miss Scott retorted: "Why should we pay an extortionate rent out of our pensions?

"We intend to remain until a suitable offer is made, even if it means staying here while they demolish our home around us."

Mrs Scott denied claims by Kesteven County Council that terms had been agreed three months earlier. A West Kesteven Rural Council spokesman said: "We offered them a house, but apparently it was at the wrong end of the village. There was little more we could do."

Heliport set to take off

GRANTHAM looked to the future, by planning to build a heliport.

A joint meeting of the town council and chambers of trade and commerce agreed that an area 40m square would be enough.

Peter Lee said the best place was Spittlegate Level, the site of Tony's Cafe, which was due to move to the north end of the Grantham bypass.

Agreeing on the site, deputy town clerk Philip Green said that it would be ideal, as it would keep the noise away from housing.

Miss jumps to it

A TEACHER jumped fully clothed into Wyndham Park swimming pool after one of her pupils got into difficulties.

Rosemary Betts leaped to the rescue of Carol Gray (7), of St Wulfram's Primary School, New Beacon Road, who lost her footing.

Carol was having her first swimming lesson and was sick through swallowing too much water.

Mrs Betts was taken to her headmaster's house in Brook Street to dry out her clothes.

Hall sold

BOOTHBY Hall, Boothby Pagnall, was sold to a man who had just returned from Argentina for £5,250.

The sale included a farmhouse, a 12th Century manor and 750 acres of cultivated land.

Bypass workers smash road-laying records

THE Grantham A1 bypass opened in October, leaving the town deserted. In an unofficial census, motor dealer Aubrey Musson of North Parade, counted 648 vehicles travelling though Great Gonerby on the Sunday before it opened.

The following week it was down to 104 vehicles including 11 lorries.

The £2 million bypass as well as taking the danger and chaos from the town, also failed to record a single accident in the first eight days.

In June, main contractors Robert McGregor established a new British record, laying 425m of carriageway in a day. This was despite a tipper lorry overturning and being put out of action for a week. Workmen reached their target with 20 minutes to spare.

Police said with less traffic in town they were able to supervise outlying villages more effectively.

Ruston takeover promises more work for town

THE takeover of Birmingham company Alfred Wiseman by Ruston and Hornsby was good news for Grantham, according to the board of directors. Grantham works manager T B Colman, said it would mean plenty more work for the London Road works.

He said: "We have ample room for expansion. There will be new lines entirely which will inject new life here.

"It means full employment will be guaranteed.

"It will replace the declining work on horizontal engines."

Swimpool is picked

A COMMITTEE charged with celebrating Grantham's Quincentenary as a borough, decided to build a £180,000 indoor swimming pool. It would have a 300-seat café and be Olympic standard.

Proposals for both a Newton university scholarship and a civic hall were rejected.

Sick man stole tree

A 26-year-old Grantham man, who had been off work sick for seven months, was fined £2 for stealing a tree.

He told Spittlegate magistrates he had not enough money for coal to keep his wife and six children warm.

He pleaded guilty to chopping down the five-metre tall hawthorn tree for firewood.

New School

GRANTHAM'S newest school, St Hugh's Secondary Modern on the Earlesfield estate, was opened by the Earl of Ancaster.

Call for brighter Newton

A TOWN councillor was rebuked for saying Newton's statue should be painted. Coun John Foster said fellow councillor John Wallwork's comments were nonsense.

He said "This is the statue of a great man, not a clown." But Mr Wallwork said his suggestion was taken out of context. He said he simply thought the statue could be in natural colours instead of looking dirty and dour.

Court closes

ONE of the country's smallest courts, Belvoir Magistrates Court, closed after 900 years. Cases were transferred to Melton Mowbray.

Van in river plunge

A VAN plunged into the River Witham from Bridge End Road bridge, after running out of control down Somerby Hill. No one was hurt.

Late drinks

DRINKERS in town were given an extra half hour at each end of the day. Licensing justices said pubs could open from 10.30am instead of 11am until 3pm during the day and from 6pm until 10.30pm instead of 10pm at night.

The new times excluded Sunday, which continued to be from noon to 2pm for lunch and 7pm to 10pm in the evening.

Off the rails

AN iron ore train came off the rails on the Belvoir line. It happened near Muston railway bridge. The private line, owned by Stewart and Lloyds, served Woolsthorpe and Harlaxton quarries.

Plane hits farmhouse

TWO women were killed when a £1million Victor bomber crashed on a farmhouse at Stubton.

Two of the five crew also died.

Although Cecily Gibson (22) and her aunt Annie Gibson (55) perished, farmer Dennis Burtt and his wife were both flung clear and escaped with pelvic and leg injuries.

Sore throat forces the Queen to cancel royal visit

THERE was disappointment when the Queen's official visit to visit the WRAF establishment at RAF Spitalgate was cancelled at the last minute. After weeks of preparation, the visit was called off at the 11th hour due to Her Majesty suffering from a sore throat. The Duchess of Gloucester deputised for her.

Only the planting of a Chinese tree of heaven was cancelled altogether.

The Duchess said: "The Queen has asked me to tell all members of the WRAF of her great regret at being unable to be with them."

New slaughter house

THE new abattoir which opened on Dysart Road in February, was described as the most modern in the midlands.

Owned by Grantham and District Butchers Association, it replaced the condemned corporation slaughterhouse in Inner Street.

Maggie rings her dad

MP for Finchley Margaret Thatcher opened the subscriber trunk dialling system (STD) in Tudor and Highgate, London, by ringing Melton Post Office. Her father, Alf Roberts, of North Parade, Grantham, was there to answer by arrangement.

Cyclist killed

GEORGE Willie Scoffin, owner of Moulds shoe shop, Watergate, was killed when his bicycle collided with a double-decker bus at the Manthorpe Road-Brook Street junction. The bus ploughed into the window of E L Simpson's grocery shop on the corner.

Cheap loans

ARTHUR Shouler of Melton Mowbray Building Society said it was untrue that you needed to earn £20 a week to afford a mortgage. He said his society would rather lend two people £1,500 for a house than one person £3,000.

Hungry truckers to pass by the bypass

LONG-distance lorry drivers were shunning the newly opened Grantham bypass and driving through town to eat at Tony's Cafe at Spittlegate Level.

So the county council gave owner Tony Wakley, of Denton Avenue, permission to move his cafe to the north end of the £2 million road.

Mr Wakley said: "It came as a shock when I discovered the road would bypass me as well as the town.

"But my regular customers made it clear they would still drive through town to come here and thus avoid the bypass."

A traffic survey revealed 30 per cent of all lorries using the Great North Road (A1) stopped at Tony's.

An earlier application for the new site was turned down but the county council decided it was a special case and he should be allowed to move. The cafe, open 24 hours a day, served up to 4,000 meals daily.

It's a twist say teenagers

GRANTHAM'S first twist competition was staged at BMARCo Social Club and organised by Huntingtower Road Allotment Association.

Dancing to the Pontiacs, one of the winning couples were Miss J Murphy and Donald Holmes (pictured) who won an electric razor and a hairdryer.

Silverware stolen

MIDLAND Bank manager Mr R G Hodge returned home to find his house burgled.

Georgian silver worth £200 was stolen.

He returned from an appointment in Nottingham to find all the drawers in every piece of furniture had been ransacked.

A small amount of cash and cigars were also taken.

Saint Wulfram's Church is worth third of a million

INSURERS valuing St Wulfram's Church said it was worth £360,000.

This left the church wondering where it would find the extra premiums which would rocket to £6 per week for the buildings and contents.

Members of the church council said they were "astonished at the astronomical figures involved."

The increases were due to storm damage on a Sheffield Church which was underinsured.

Insurers put the value of the church building at £250,000.

They said the organ was worth £25,000, the bells £8,500, the windows £33,000 and the altar reredos £1,000.

The communion plate was worth only £400. This was less than in 1808 when the plate was stolen and 100 guineas reward was unsuccessfully offered for its return.

Grantham in the News 1963

Queen Mum's visit puts icing on the quin year cake

The Queen Mother with Grantham Mayor Ron Briggs.

A VISIT by the Queen Mother was the high spot of Grantham's Quincentenary celebrations.

Of all the events to celebrate the 500th anniversary of the borough charter, Her Majesty's visit was the most memorable.

Her day began at Leadenham, where the Royal train stayed overnight.

After arriving at Grantham station, she was taken to a reception at the Guildhall.

There, she was presented with a bouquet by the Mayor's daughter, 14-year-old Lynda Briggs. Her brother Christopher missed the big day, sitting his GCE exams. After a visit to Grantham Hospital and a reception from 6,000 enthusiastic children at Wyndham Park, she opened Chandos House old people's home, Gorse Road. She also called at Grantham College for a cup of tea.

New fire station to be built

THE Kesteven Fire Brigade headquarters, Harlaxton Road, was due to be demolished and a new one built on the site.

Brigade bosses decided that the building, erected just after the war, was no longer fit for its purpose. The firemen in the picture include Gordon Walmsley, Dick Joynes, Eric Wright, Pete Brewin, Vernon Gilbard, Sub Officer Hemfrey and Bert Hutchins.

Uncle Harry retires

HARRY Sanders, manager of the Granada cinema since 1937, retired. He was a popular figure in the town and known to tens of thousands of youngsters as Uncle Harry through the Granadiers' Saturday morning cinema club He was also held in high esteem by teenagers, several of whom he put on the road to stardom with his Sunday talent nights.

These included ITV's Drumbeat host Vince Eager (Grantham lad Roy Taylor) and Shadows guitarist Brian Locking.

Mr Sanders also discovered Freddie Bartholomew, who went on to star in Hollywood. Mr Sanders began his career in Maesteg, Wales.

Last blast for steam engine

ONE of the last steam locomotives was sold by British Railways to a Grantham scrap metal dealer.

It made one last whistle blast before the furnace closed.

Built in Doncaster in 1941, the 120-tonne loco 63982 was shunted into the sidings of F C Larkinson, of Dysart Road for breaking. The wheels alone weigh four tonnes and five tonnes was non-ferrous metals.

Most of the steel was sent to Birmingham for resmelting.

Child's play

A RETIRED eight-tonne steam engine became the latest addition to Wyndham Park playing field.

Presented by chairman of Eddison Plant Hire, Raymond Birch, the 41-year-old was given a new lease of life as playground equipment. Steps were added for access and moving parts immobilised. It was built by Aveling Porter, of Kent. The company once owned 500 steam rollers but they had all been replaced by diesel-powered ones.

Sticky wicket

CRICKETERS at Threekingham were forced to scatter when a glider landed on their pitch during a match against Folkingham.

Players were greeted by a cheery pilot who said: "Sorry chaps, it was the only place to make a forced landing."

Spectators helped move the glider for the match to continue.

The pilot watched the match and joined players for interval tea.

Seven-metre drifts

ROADS around Grantham were blocked as the area was in the grip of Siberian conditions.

Gale force winds drifted snow to seven metres on the A607 between Harlaxton and Waltham-on-the-Wolds. Light vehicles cut across fields at Croxton Kerrial to avoid the drifts. It was the longest cold spell since the 1890s.

Lack of power

GREAT Gonerby was without electricity for 24 hours during arctic conditions.

Many Grantham homes were also affected, due to icing on the overhead powerlines.

Fire at the Red Lion

A MYSTERY blaze broke out at the Red Lion Hotel, High Street, once one of the town's most popular public houses. But the building's fate was already sealed as it was already being demolished.

It was making way for a modern shopping development. Other buildings being pulled down included the alms houses and the former gas showroom. The new scheme included new showrooms for East Midlands Electricity Board and East Midlands Gas Board.

Driverless lorry runs into council house

A RUNAWAY coal lorry caused hundreds of pounds in damage to a council house.

The vehicle. owned by Parson Bros and Snape, was parked at the top of Melbourne Road when it began to move downhill. It struck a car on the way, forcing it across the road where it demolished a telegraph pole. It crossed the green and became wedged at the side of the house occupied by the Jackson family.

Mr Jackson said he was having lunch when he heard scraping noises and the tiles began to fall from the roof.

He said: "I got a bigger shock when there was no driver in it."

Eight-year-old David Guy who lived next door saw it all.

He said: "The telegraph post shot into the air and the lorry came straight for the houses."

No one was hurt in the incident.

Children snatched from blazing home

NEIGHBOURS braved smoke-filled rooms to rescue three children when a fire broke out in Ryde Avenue. Twins Lorraine and Stephen Bailey (3) and Trevor (2) were taken to Grantham Hospital and discharged after treatment. Six-month-old baby Clive was snatched from a burning settee by his mother.

He was taken to Nottingham City Hospital and described as being "as good as can be expected".

Mrs Bailey had left the house for a few minutes and returned to find the living room full of smoke.

Neighbours Mrs Calvert and Mr Tuffs were alerted by cries for help.

Town gets Home visit

SIR Alex Douglas Home became the third Prime Minister to visit Grantham since the war.

He rounded off the visit with an address to a packed audience at Grantham College.

Well over 1,000 people turned out to hear the Premier's first speech since returning from the USA three days earlier.

He visited Aveling Barford in the morning, accompanied by Grantham MP Joe Godber.

There he chatted with workmen and drove a road roller.

House sense

THE average borrower with the Melton Mowbray Building Society had a mortgage of £1,510, shareholders were told at the annual meeting.

The assets of the small society with a branch on Grantham High Street, stood at £3.7 million, £250,000 up on the previous year,

Only three mortgage holders were in arrears, a total of £349.

Glamour

JENNIFER Wilkinson (centre) was voted Grantham Quincentenary Queen to celebrate the 500th anniversary of the borough charter. In second place was Pamela Dixon, (left) with Susan Hurst third.

Back to work

AFTER a record-breaking 30 weeks strike, Aveling Barford draughtsmen returned to work.

An undisclosed offer was made by management which the 76 strikers accepted.

The action, which cost the company £1,000 per week, was in support of a claim to bring their wages into line with the DATA minimum rates.

Out of steam

STEAM locomotives, which had run through Grantham for more than a century, were taken out of commission.

But it was not all gloom.

The 70 railwaymen who expected to be laid off were transferred to work on the new diesel locos. Some moved to Peterborough.

Population

GRANTHAM'S population had risen by 1,493 to 25,048 in 10 years.

Drapers' demise

GRANTHAM draper G W Green, closed after 52 years. The premises, 49-51 High Street, was taken over by national lingerie chain Dorothy Perkins.

Tidy station

GRANTHAM Railway station was second in the British Railways Eastern Region best-kept station competition.

The winner was Colchester with Liverpool Street, London, third.

Cold comfort

FREEZING householders were told coal was on a three-week waiting list, following a rush when winter began early.

Merchant George Foster said six weeks earlier there had been stockpiles which they could scarcely give away.

Hot jumpers

KESTEVEN County Council agreed to spend £30 on pullovers for firemen.

Deal on wheels

KESTEVEN County Council decided not to go ahead with the anticipated increased fees for the Meals on Wheels service.

It was planned to rise to 6.2p but it remained at 5p, as it was when introduced in 1954.

In the same period, pensions went up £1.25 per week.

King's School is "horrible" say education chiefs

CONDITIONS at Grantham King's School were described as "scandalous, disturbing and horrible" in a report to the Education Minister, Sir Edward Boyle.

A report by the Campaign for Education spelled out the school's shortcomings.

The 16th Century part was used as an assembly hall.

Boys were packed in so tightly, they could hardly hold a hymn book.

Classrooms were so overcrowded, some pupils could not see the blackboard. Wooden huts, built in 1919, were still in use as classrooms, even though they had been declared unfit in 1948.

One-third of the 540 boys did not get physical training because the assembly hall had to double for both PT and music.

Both had to be cancelled at examination time.

Learners a danger

TWO headteachers said they were worried about road safety around their schools, due to danger from learner drivers.

They said the L-drivers were reversing into the busy cul-de-sac where there were the exits to two schools.

Mr A T Storey of Springfield Secondary School, and Herbert Pacey, of Huntingtower Road School, said they practice three-point turns from 9am every day. Mr Pacey said the previous day, six learners performed the manoeuvre in 90 minutes.

He said: "There are a dozen more suitable sites. Why pick on this one?

"They often mount the kerb. It's an accident waiting to happen."

Grantham in the News 1964

Big bang signals the end of steam

ON a cold January day, British Rail blew up the coaling tower, which fuelled the steam locomotives.

The railway yards, which once employed more than 1,000 men, were being run down and the coaling tower was redundant. It stood on the site later occupied by the canning factory, Springfield Road

Peter Nicholls, who took the picture said: "It was done in secret for safety reasons. They didn't want a crowd.

"But at 8am, when it was due, it was thick fog. The contractors had to wait until 2pm for it to clear."

Then, with the press of a button, the tower which had been a landmark since 1937 came crashing down.

Teenagers claim town is dying on its feet

GRANTHAM was lagging behind towns with more dynamic leadership. That was the view of the majority of town teenagers who entered an essay writing competition organised by Grantham Civic Trust.

They said it is inefficient as a shopping centre and the council has no will to "grasp the nettle".

Nearly all the entrants criticised the borough's inadequate recreation facilities and many say the proposed indoor swimming pool was a case where money could have been better spent.

King's School student A J Basker (17) said: "Grantham is letting itself be overtaken by other towns with more dynamic forces behind them.

"I think it will be very difficult to break down Grantham lethargy in the matter of redevelopment.

"I guess if I return in 10 years time I will find the town changed in only minor aspects

"There will probably be an increase in broken windows and gravel parking spaces."

St Hugh's School pupil Alan Bryan (16) said: "The town centre needs seeing to.

"It looks as if it's just about falling down."

Adjudicators Dr F A Webster and K R Fennell of the county planning department described the young-sters' views as "disturbing".

Sutch's life

SCREAMING Lord Sutch, the pop star who fought Labour Party leader Harold Wilson at the General Election, was filming in Grantham. It was a documentary about his life, recorded for BBC2. Viewers able to get the channel saw him sending local teenagers into a frenzy with his act at the Rhythm and Blues Face Club, London Road.

Top nurse

GRANTHAM nurse Belinda Roe won both the Griffin Silver Buckle and the Matron's prize at Grantham Hospital and Hill View Hospital Schools of Nursing prize-giving. She received the award from KGGS old girl Margaret Thatcher MP.

Plucky Jim

GRANTHAM Town FC beat Sutton Town 6-2 in the Midland League. Player manager Jimmy Rayner scored all six for Town.

No takers

GRANTHAM Youth Centre, New Beacon Road, which cost ratepayers £25,000, remained closed as the council was unable to find a leader.

The post carried a yearly salary of £730 rising to £1,140 but no one wanted the job.

Mystery staircase found

BUILDERS and decorators working on the King's Room (or La Chambre du Roi) at the Angel and Royal Hotel discovered a hitherto unknown stone, spiral staircase.

It was hidden by hessian and plaster.

Earlier, in 1957, workman discovered a nine-foot wide 14th Century fireplace in a front bar which had been hidden for hundreds of years.

High prices

TWO High Street properties came under the hammer at a London auction, fetching £81,000.

The sites of the former almshouses and the Georgian building next door, occupied for many years by Mr Wallace's dental practice, had outline permission for redevelopment as four shops with offices or flats above. The sale was at the London Auction Mart.

Hill View Hospital moves

FORTY-four chronically sick patients were moved from Hill View Hospital, Dysart Road, to a new ward at the General Hospital, Manthorpe Road.

Hill View was to close once the new maternity wing at Grantham Hospital was complete, putting all patients on one site.

Ancaster Roman grave digs upsets the locals

FAMILIES in Ancaster were furious following archaeological excavations in the village cemetery.

The archaeologists from Nottingham University removed several Roman skeletons, digging within inches of recent graves.

Villagers said it was overstepping the mark to remove remains from consecrated grounds.

A widow who saw a four-metre pit next to her husband's four-year-old grave and two skeletons nearby, almost fainted at the sight She said: "I was horrified."

Trapped by beam

A MAN was trapped by a two-tonne beam during demolition work at the former Harrison's basket factory, behind R H Neal.

Fortunately the cranemakers quickly supplied a 4.5 tonne hydraulic crane for his rescue.

Self-employed Edward Charlton was taken by ambulance to Grantham Hospital with a suspected broken ankle.

Takeover

CRANEMAKERS R H Neal merged with two other companies to become part of British Crane Corporation. Managing director of the Dysart Road works, C S Shaw, said the development could only be good news for the workforce.

Blow me

HUNDREDS of soldiers were called to clear unexploded bombs from a popular picnic site. More than 50 bombs were found at Eager Lodge Farm at Swinstead.

Head bans ex-pupil with Beatle haircut

A MANTHORPE youth, who left King's School the previous year with six GCE O-levels, was barred from receiving his certificate at the annual speech night at the Drill Hall, because of his hairstyle.

Although allowed in the hall to watch, he was told he could not collect his certificate. John Dickinson (18) an apprentice draughtsman with Aveling Barford, was invited to the ceremony and accepted. But when he reached the door, one of the masters told him he could not collect his award due to his Beatle haircut. His parents said: "It may be long but he was smartly dressed in the latest fashion."

Headmaster G A Goodban said he supported the master's action.

He said: "It's a question of suitability."

Wage demand

FOLKINGHAM branch of the National Farmworkers Union demanded a £2 per week rise to bring the wage to £12 for a 40-hour week.

Rise in Jobless

SEVENTY adults were found work by Grantham Labour Exchange in January. This left 82 adult vacancies unfilled.

The total out of work rose from 273 the previous month to 319: 209 men, 14 boys, 82 women and 14 girls.

Engaging number

WORK began on the new STD (subscriber trunk dialling) telephone exchange in Inner Street.

The old manual exchange at the General Post Office, St Peter's Hill, was at bursting point as subscribers had reached 2,250.

Umbrellas down

THE umbrella factory which opened on London Road about 20 years earlier, closed.

Production was transferred to the firm's Leicester factory.

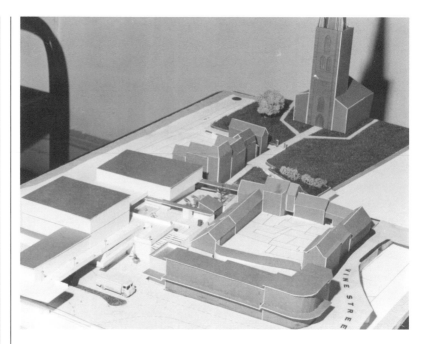

Grantham's blueprint for development

A THREE-dimensional model and a site plan for the future of Watergate was put before Grantham town councillors.

They showed an inner ring road at the bottom of Watergate and a two-tier construction with offices or shops bridging the road.

There was also a covered shopping precinct.

Coun Lloyd Ramsden said although the proposals would take many years to put into effect, the younger generation would benefit.

County planning officer Brian Bell said Grantham should be looking at a shopping catchment area of up to 100,000 shoppers. He said Grantham was ideal for expansion and foresaw a population of 60,000. Mr Bell said the main areas for town centre development were the Broad Street, Swinegate and Watergate area; the lower end of Westgate, Welby Street and Wharf Road area, 'University Square', and the East Street area.

He said: "St Wulfram's Church is the only dominant building in the town centre. The policy should allow for some tall buildings in strategic positions."

He said pedestrians should have absolute preference in shopping areas and the street system re-designed for convenient access and service.

"High Street and Market Place should become a pedestrian precinct," he said.

New boss is a record breaker

CENTRE forward Terry Bly (28), known for his goal-scoring feats with Norwich City, Peterborough United and Coventry City, signed as Grantham Town FC's player-manager.

A year previously, Notts County paid £13,000 for the player but he had failed to settle. County's attack was spearheaded by former Grantham manager Jim Rayner.

After selling Rayner to County for £2,500, Grantham bought Bly for a 'four-figure sum'.

With Peterborough, he scored a record-breaking 52 League goals.

Crematorium

A MODEL of the new crematorium was unveiled by the council. It was planned to build it at the cemetery, Harrowby Road.

Height fine

A JOINERY company was fined £10 for allowing two of its workers at Dowsby to work on scaffolding two metres high without guardrails.

End for Mansion

WEST Willoughby Hall, near Ancaster, was demolished by Lincoln explosives experts. The house built by the Hitchcock family in 1875 had been closed for 30 years and at one stage became a fertiliser factory. It was used by the military during the Second World War. Plans to demolish the building several years ago fell through and the shell became a hazard. The land on which it stood was bought by farmer Peter Murray, who wanted the land for agriculture.

The Ancaster stone was sold and the site cleared within two months.

1965 Grantham in the News

New school to replace the former Girls' Central

WALTON Girls' School, built to replace the Girls Central, was completed at the end of the year.

The old school, in Castlegate, dating from 1920 just didn't come up to scratch.

Work began in a field off Kitty Briggs Lane and within two years the four-storey structure was open.

The 300 girls were delighted with their new light and airy premises.

The Girls' Central had been dark with outside toilets across the playground from the main building.

It was so poorly designed, visitors wanting to see the headmistress, the formidable Nina Hewitt, had to go through a classroom to her office.

The old school only had two headteachers in its history, Miss Jabet, who retired in 1946 and Miss Hewitt who took over from her. Miss Hewitt was appointed the first headteacher of Walton Girls.

Walkers' passing out parade at Drill Hall

FORTY girls fainted and had to be carried out when hundreds of screaming teenagers gave the Walker Brothers the noisiest reception any act had seen in Grantham.

The American group was appearing at the Drill Hall, Sandon Road. The girls were carried over the stage as the brothers' backing group played.

At one stage the brothers refused to appear, fearing for their safety.

Such was the frenzy whipped up, the chart toppers' act had to be abandoned after 15 minutes.

John, Scott and Gary sang their hit Make it Easy on Yourself during their brief session, but could hardly be heard through the crescendo of screams.

Security men formed a ring of steel in front of the stage but several girls managed to breach it. One ripped the shirt from Scott's back as he sang. The brothers were trapped in their dressing room for more than an hour afterwards. Minders then formed a chain at the back of the building and the stars made a dash for their American Cadillac.

Barkston twins are born miles apart

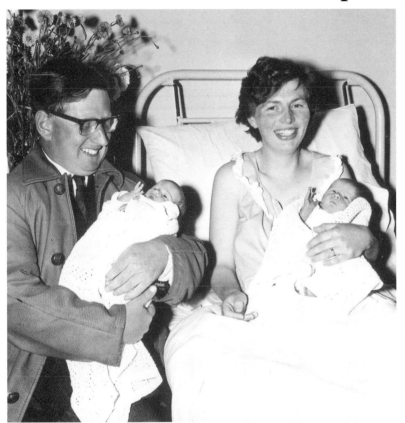

MINUTES after a Barkston mum gave birth to a baby daughter at Grantham Hospital, she was taken to Nottingham City Hospital where a second was born.

Farmer's wife Susan Watson, 24, was taken 24 miles by ambulance after complications set in.

Mrs Watson and her husband Richard called the Lincolnshire twin Judith Louise and the Nottinghamshire twin Sally Ann.

She was reunited with the second daughter in Grantham two days later.

The couple, who also had an 18 month-old daughter Jacqueline, were married in 1962.

Burglars have a ball while police dance the night away

RED-faced policemen were faced with detecting six shop burglaries on the night of their annual ball at the Guildhall.

The thieves stole only small amounts of cash in each case.

They broke into greengrocers A G Towers, fishmonger Mrs A Morrison, EMEB, Heriot's bakery, estate agents W H Brown, and builders merchants Arthur Syddall.

Pool site agreed again

THE site of Grantham's indoor swimming pool was fixed. Grantham Quincentenary Memorial Committee scrapped plans for both Stonebridge Close and Beaconfield in favour of Wyndham Park. Borough councillors agreed the site of the park's outdoor pool was the best place for it.

No to petrol

AN application by Wilcancis Properties to build a petrol filling station in Welby Street was turned down by the borough council. They said it would create unsatisfactory traffic conditions.

Fell from factory roof

A PLUMBER fell 10m from the roof of Alfred Wiseman's factory, London Road – and carried on working.

David Mabletoft, 24. broke a bone in his foot – and that was the extent of his injuries.

Firemen stuck in drift

CORBY Glen firefighters on their way to a farm blaze at Ingoldsby got stuck in a snow drift 3km from their destination.

They dug themselves out and returned to base while their Grantham colleagues put out the fire.

Talking rubbish

CHIEF public health officer M E Johnson told borough councillors refuse collections should be made weekly. He said the current practice of fortnightly collections was not good enough.

Headmistress retires

MISS Dorothy Gillies retired as headmistress of Kesteven and Grantham Girls' School after 25 years.

Bread queues

QUEUES of a size not seen since the end of the Second World War formed outside town bakeries.

An acute bread shortage was caused by a strike of Nottingham bread van drivers.

Local bakers tried to satisfy demand but ran out of yeast.

No band – no parade

FOR the first time since RAF Spitalgate was awarded the freedom of the borough in 1952, there was no Battle of Britain parade through Grantham.

Instead, 120 personnel went by bus from the camp to St Wulfram's for the service and were driven back again.

A Defence Ministry spokesman said no bands were available.

Out of Cup but rewards are a knockout

GRANTHAM FC's ground record was smashed by 110, when 6,257 spectators turned out to watch them play Swindon Town in the FA Cup.

The second round match beat the London Road record set against Ilkeston in 1947.

Although the team lost 6-1 to the Third Division side, it ended a seven-match run which included five excellent home gates.

It was the first time Grantham had got that far in the competition since playing Wigan in 1928.

On average 3,438 watched the home cup ties, and 1,432 watched home league matches during the run. Town hit 28 cup goals, including nine from centre forward Mike Alexander and six from player-manager Terry Bly.

Picture shows director Frank Baxter and an FA official inspecting the temporary staging for the Swindon match.

One boy jobless

ALL but one of the Easter leavers were found work by June. Grantham and Sleaford unemployment committee said the one boy out of 259 leavers would soon find work. Secretary T B Colman said many of the July leavers had already found work in advance. He said: "It's very pleasing."

Standby for a water shortage

RESIDENTS in Harrowby and Cherry Orchard had to queue for water from a 500-gallon tanker when supplies were hit by a cracked water main. These people are on Harrowby Lane on a chilly and windy February day.

Time at Carlton Scroop

HELEN Humphrey called "Time" for the very last time at the Coach and Horses, Carlton Scroop. Brewers Stewart and Pattinson closed the pub the next day. Miss Humphrey had been landlady since the end of the war.

Long distance

TWO dozen St Hugh's School pupils living in Great Gonerby had a 90 minute daily trip to school. Their bus, which started in the village, went on a 20-mile route including Hough-on-the Hill and Barkston, picking up other children along the way.

Bathrooms banned

PERMISSION to install kitchens, toilets and bathrooms in Dawson's Almshouses, Brook Street, was refused by the borough council because of a by-law.

Lorries on increase

THE number of lorries going through Grantham had quadrupled over the past 10 year. Deputy county planning office Dr K R Fennell said: "It is estimated there are 1,700 vehicles come into Grantham every hour, underlining the urgency for planning a road system in the town."

Team told: You can't change on the bus

FED up of changing behind the hedgerow, a Grantham soccer team were delighted when they were offered a single-decker bus to change in.

But borough councillors were less enthusiastic.

They told the players of Beeden Park FC they could not leave the bus on the Meres recreation ground.

Club secretary T. Atter said: "Some of the changing rooms up here are a disgrace. In fact they all are except St John's."

The club played friendly matches on Sunday, hiring St Anne's FC pitch for 50p a match.

He said: "Next season we start playing in a Sunday league.

"Teams that play us will expect something a bit better than a hedge.

"It's all right in summer but it's cold up there in winter."

Parks committee chairman Harry Haworth said he believed the bus would be a dangerous attraction for children and would soon become derelict.

Residents want gun test ban

HOUSEHOLDERS in the Denton Avenue area were calling on Bmarco's firing range to be closed.

They said testing the guns in the company's tunnel was noisy and could damage their foundations.

Norah Potter of Walton Gardens , said: "It nearly shakes you off your feet. It's dreadful." Her husband Cyril, a postman, said he cannot sleep in the afternoon.

It's Boots

A HIGH Street store which began three years ago as a Fine Fare supermarket was bought by Boots. It was built on the site of the Horse and Jockey pub.

Boots planned to shut its two branches and combine them at the new premises.

Shops vote for day off

GRANTHAM traders voted for a five-day week.

By 33 votes to seven, they decided to close all day on Wednesdays, replacing the early closing on afternoons.

Ald Len Audus said: "We are open 50 hours a week. That is not good for the employees."

But not everyone was in favour.

Baker F J Webster said: "Some of the big boys are going to be a big danger. You are putting a nail in your own coffins."

Hunter dies at Staunton Show

TRAGEDY struck at the Staunton Show when a horse ridden by Jim Webster and owned by Lord Belper, collapsed with a heart attack.

The hunter died during the Belvoir Hunt's parade of hounds.

Mr Webster fell with his left leg under the horse and was taken to hospital.

It's the boys who take the biscuit at pastry making

AN experiment begun two years before at Swayfield School proved children aged five could be taught to cook.

But the biggest surprise at the 28-pupil school was that boys were better at it than girls.

Headmistress Sheena Kelly, said: "Funnily enough, the boys' pastry always turns out the best. The girls get furious about it.

"I began the cookery lessons because it is a practical way of teaching weights and measures. They also learn hygiene and domestic science although they are not allowed to use the oven."

The children were allowed to take their finished work to their parents but most of them ate it on the way home."

Refuse to pay TV fee says councillor

A COUNCILLOR has told Grantham residents to refuse to pay their TV licences until they got better reception.

Coun Tom Scott had sent a 1,000-page petition to the Postmaster General and was angered by the reply.

Mr Scott said: "The BBC admits that reception deteriorates, especially in the summer.

"It said something will be done when Belmont opens next year but it means buying new aerials.

"Why should we have to pay for a service we can't get and pay even more in the hope of improving it? "I am certainly not happy with this reply."

Council is out of tune

A COLSTERWORTH woman who had been a musician for 70 years was told by councillors she could not have a small piano in her council flat.

West Kesteven District Council refused permission because they said her Newton Court flat was too small. But Helen Foster, 82, said the authority was being silly.

She said: "Surely it's up to me to decide whether I've got room. Having a piano is more important to me than anything.

"If the flat is too small I'll get rid of something else. I wouldn't make as much noise as a TV."

Before moving to the flat two years before, Mrs Foster was known as the piano-playing licensee of the village's George Hotel.

Clerk to the council J B Morgan said: "We want tenants to have as many of their own things as possible but a small piano could lead to a big piano and so on."

Mill on the market

SWALLOW'S Mill owners decided to sell the property after nearly 50 years.

The century-old company announced the Bridge End Road building would be put on the market. Work was transferred to its Gonerby grain store. Agents said the property was ideal for offices or an entertainment venue.

1966 Grantham in the News

Campaign against Spittlegate Gipsy site

Councillors visit the proposed travellers' site on Spittlgate Hill.

ANGRY residents in St John's ward began a fight against a proposed Gipsy caravan site on Spittlegate Hill. They handed in a 130-name petition to the town clerk protesting at the plan.

The storm erupted the previous Monday when 80 people attended a meeting of the ward Labour Party to protest over the proposals for land at the top of Stamford Street.

Coun Elstone said: "Property values in Victoria Street will be depreciated for a start.

"Then there's the traffic hazard created by vehicles going in and out of the site. "

Tory councillor Tom Scott said: "I shall fight this by all constitutional means and oppose it tooth and nail.

"We've been 20 years trying to get a playing field for the area yet they can find a caravan site just like that."

Councillors agreed and the health committee threw out the proposals, favouring a site at Sheepwash Lane, Barrowby.

Chairman Ernest Smith said: "As far as the borough council is concerned this proposal is washed out. It was absolutely ridiculous."

About turn on toilets

THE borough council had second thoughts about charging Grantham FC £25 rent for the public toilets to be built on London Road. It followed a letter from the club saying it had not been consulted.

Ancient monument could be lost forever

WORK on the 13th Century Knights Templar site at South Witham could be abandoned for the want of £200.

And that was despite £4,000 having been spent already, including excavations on a site prior to the Norman Conquest,

Requests for the money from the Ministry of Works suggested the cash had dried up.

Archaeologists said this was one of the most important sites of its kind. But instead of being preserved it was to be bulldozed and redeveloped.

Great Gonerby unholy row may lead to closure of both chapels

A FEUD between two Methodist churches at Great Gonerby over which building should close, was likely to end with them both being shut down.

Superintendent Minister, the Rev J Ewart Shepherd, said there was a bitter rivalry between the churches at Spring End and Green Street.

He said: "It's a very sad story.

"It's simply open antagonism between two church bodies who are worshipping their buildings.

"We have tried to get them both together but they will not."

The rivalry began 20 years earlier when an architect's report urged Green Street Chapel should close.

Ever since, Green Street supporters had fought the proposal.

Attempts to break the deadlock had failed and Mr Shepherd said there was little chance of agreement for amalgamation.

At Christmas, the two chapels held competing services, with those supporting one refusing to attend the other.

Mr Shepherd said this left only a handful of worshippers at each.

He said: "It doesn't seem possible for there to be such open antagonism in these days of enlightenment."

Super houses but no one can afford them

COMBINED rent and rates on 90 homes being built on the Earlesfield estate could be as much as £6 per week, Grantham councillors were told.

It was calculated after news that the lowest tender received for building them was £266,070.

There were sighs of shock from the public gallery as Coun John Wallwork revealed the news.

He said; "I'm very perturbed about the situation. This sum is fantastic." Coun Tom Scott added: "This is far above what Grantham people can afford to pay."

But Coun Lloyd Ramsden said the dwellings were "super houses" which were larger and had more amenities than usual.

"If people want a super council house then the people who want them will have to pay more," he said.

Ship strike hits church

THE national seamen's strike unfortunately hit a four-day Whitsun flower festival planned by St Wulfram's Church.

Hot weather left local blooms in short supplies so flower arrangers had to look to Jersey and the continent.

Organiser Mr W J C Gregory said: "It's a headache.

"Looking overseas has put costs up by 25 per cent. Now the strike leaves us struggling to get them."

Wrong treatment?

TYRE remoulders Vacu-Lug made a formal complaint against Grantham Hospital saying it gave one of its employees the wrong treatment.

The 29-year-old was injured when a tyre weighing 900kg fell on his leg. Casualty staff gave him a cold compress, a splint and later a plaster cast.

A hospital spokesman said they would await the findings of an inquiry.

Cold comfort

PUPILS at the Boys' Central School, Hill Avenue, were forced to change for sport in a room one degree above freezing.

Ald Albert Bellamy asked Kesteven Education committee to splash out £100 on electric heaters for the youngsters.

Jobless rising

THE number of people out of work rose to 335 in October, although Labour Exchange manager Norman Lenton said he thought it had peaked. There were 230 men, 71 women, 22 boys and 12 girls unemployed.

Mr Lenton said: "It is the highest for many years but I didn't expect it to rise so meteorically."

Yanks a lot

A PARTY of 80 American students arrived at Harlaxton Manor, being the first batch from Stanford University, California, which transformed the former stately home into its British campus.

Confusion as one way system comes to town

CONFUSION reigned as one-way streets were introduced to Grantham's town centre. Motorists were faced with No Entry signs, where they had previously driven unchallenged and just didn't know where to turn next. Castlegate, Elmer Street, Blue Gate and Finkin Street all became part of the new system to ease traffic flow.

On St Peter's Hill (pictured), which was unchanged, motorists were left scratching their heads, wondering which way to go. Police seemed equally confused on how to sort out the mess.

A council spokesman said: "It will be fine once people get used to it. It's only teething troubles."

Housing drive fails

THREE directors associated with Hunt Lea Estate housing development, off Harlaxton Road, were told they were extravagant at Derby bankruptcy court.

They admitted deficiencies of £98,000, £29,000 and £24,500 respectively. They agreed the cause of the company's collapse was "Mismanagement, misuse of the company's assets and blatant extravagance."

Among the excesses were financing a motor racing team which was entered into the Le Mans race with one of management as a driver.

Rocking in the wind

MASONS were called to the Market Cross in 1966 after it was reported to be 'swaying in the wind'. A giant crane was used to remove the top stones and rebuild them.

Death of Lady Brownlow

LADY Dorothy Carlotta Brownlow, wife of Lord Brownlow, died at the couple's London home in Eaton Square. Lady Brownlow (57) had received major surgery a month before and had been reported to be progressing well. The couple married in Las Vegas, USA, in 1954. It was her fifth marriage. She was cremated in London.

Chapel tower demolished

WORKMEN dismantled the tower on the Bridge End Road Wesleyan Church, which closed at Christmas 1964.

The church began as a meeting house in an Inner Street cottage and the building was erected in 1875 on land bought and donated by William Hornsby.

An assembly hall was added at the turn of the century to accommodate the largest Sunday school in the neighbourhood.

Numbers declined following the demolition of houses in Inner Street.

The main building was bought by Matt Bland for redevelopment.

Making a point

MEMBERS of Caythorpe Women's Institute were supplied with special plastic caps to slip over their stiletto heels when using the village hall.

Dream debut

ANCASTER outside left Dennis Butters made a dream debut for Grantham FC. He scored once and made four in Grantham's 5-2 win over Belper. He was signed from Grantham St Johns.

Seventh-Day school

THE Seventh-Day Adventist Church asked for planning permission to erect a new church and school in Broad Street, Grantham.

Burning desire

GRANTHAM crematorium was dedicated by the Bishop of Lincoln, the Rt Rev Kenneth Riches. It cost £52,000.

Godber scrapes back

CONSERVATIVE Joe Godber retained the Grantham seat with a greatly reduced majority.

He defeated Labour's Mary Large by a majority of 2,158, compared to nearly 6,000 at the 1964 General Election.

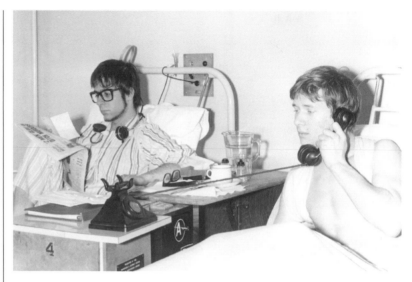

Pop fans jam phones

PHONE lines at Grantham Hospital were red hot after anxious fans heard five members of pop group Manfred Mann were taken there. Staff were swamped with calls for 48 hours, continuing after the last member of the group had left.

The musicians were taken to hospital following an accident at Long Bennington as they returned from a gig at Hull.

Leader Manfred Mann (25) and singer Paul Jones (23) were detained for observation after X-rays. Mann had a chest injury and Jones a broken collar bone. Tom MacGuinness (24), Henry Lowther (24) and Michael Hugg (25), were discharged after treatment. Driver Anthony Hales was unhurt.

Paul Jones said: "We were all asleep. I suddenly woke up and saw we were on the pavement heading for a telegraph pole.

"The car skidded round and hit a lorry on a garage forecourt."

The singer appeared on television the following day, his arm in a sling.

Nursery closed due to dysentery outbreak

A GRANTHAM day nursery was closed following an outbreak of dysentery.

Once the infection was discovered, senior medical officer Dr Elizabeth Whitely ordered the building to be shut immediately.

She said: "There is no need for parents to be alarmed.

"Not one of the children is very ill, but we took this step to stop it spreading."

She said the decision to close was not unanimous.

She said: "It is unfair to put the decision as to whether the child should be sent here or not on the mother's shoulders, so I am making it."

Hollies take town by storm

ONE of Britain's top pop groups, The Hollies, went 'like a bomb' at the Drill Hall, Sandon Road.

Youngsters poured in to see the top group and were packed shoulder to shoulder in the auditorium. Fans were treated to all the old favourites and a preview of their latest disc I Can't Let Go.

Stuck in the box

A SEVEN-year-old boy from Queensway was freed by firefighters after getting his hand stuck in a pillar box as he posted a letter on Princess Drive.

Frankie pops in

HUNDREDS of housewives turned out to see popular singer Frankie Vaughan when he opened John Wallwork's new Castlegate furniture store. He spent some time chatting to his fans.

Wiseman made loss so Ruston sells it for £24m

RUSTON and Hornsby, which included Grantham-based, Alfred Wiseman was taken over by English Electric in a £24,000,000 deal in October.

The engineering giant was keen on the merger to increase the diesel engine side of its business, making it the biggest in Britain.

The new bosses said that although the new company strategy had to be finalised, there were no plans for job losses.

Earlier in the year, it was revealed that Wiseman's had made a loss of £100,000.

Ruston and Hornsby chairman J F Mallabar said the order books at the Grantham subsidiary was 'unbalanced'.

He said improvements were unsatisfactory and turnover dropped.

He said the completion of British Rail's programme of changing from steam to diesel had much to do with a downturn.

He said; "This vacuum is proving difficult to fill with other suitable work."

Cup glory

GRANTHAM earned a second round FA Cup tie with Oldham Athletic after beating Southern Leaguers Wimbledon 2-1, at London Road. Winger Roy South scored the winning goal.

Funds up

ASSETS at Grantham Building Society rose by £49,520 to £285,379. The 161 mortgage holders borrowed an average £1,500 each at 6.75 per cent. During the year, £65,700 was loaned to 27 new homebuyers.

Green cuts red tape

FANS turned out in force to see TV personality Hughie Green open Kentons furnishing store on High Street. The star of Opportunity Knocks and Double Your Money, reportedly earning £70,000 a year, cut the red tape and signed autographs.

Avoided disaster

A MECHANICAL defect caused the fire in the cab of a lorry which was carrying 18,000 litres of petrol.
It happened on the A1 just north of Tony's Cafe.

Prompt action by the driver and firefighters soon brought it under control.

Widow told marriage was bigamous

A WIDOW was told at an inquest, her dead husband had a wife and family in Scotland.

It was revealed at the inquest of her lorry driver husband.

She said: "I was very surprised.

"I knew my husband had been married before but he said she was dead."

The shock news was revealed by the dead man's father.

Antique shop is wrecked by truck

A PASSENGER was killed when a 16-wheeler coke lorry ploughed into his family car. Horace Smart, of Harrowby Lane, was thrown from the car as the lorry smashed into Muriel Redmile's antique shop, on the corner of Bridge End Road. The shop was demolished by the impact and the bulk of the antiques were destroyed The lorry driver was freed by firefighters as part of the concrete roof fell on him.

Mrs Redmile said afterwards: "It's the sort of thing you expect when the bombs are falling but not now." Thirty men and six breakdown vehicles were used to clear the wreckage.

Students clean up with Tollemache

COUNCILLORS refused to clean up a statue on St Peter's Hill.

The request came from Lyonel Tollemache whose great-great-great uncle Frederick's statue had stood outside the Co-operative stores since 1896.

Councillors said if Mr Tollemache thought it was dirty then he could arrange to have it cleaned at his expense. Ald Stanley Richardson disagreed.

He said: "If we do want it, we should wash it. It is a disgrace."

But Grantham College students came to the rescue and gave the statue a wash and brush and collecting £25 for charity as they did.

Girls perched on the roof of a van

TWO young girls climbed on to the roof of a van parked in Edinburgh Road. But when it moved off and turned a lefthand bend, they fell off on to the road.

One received head and hand injuries, the other was unscathed.

But their prank led to a £5 fine for the 19-year-old driver.

Supt Travis told Grantham magistrates: "There was no roof rack on top of this van and their perch was precarious."

The driver said he was aware they had climbed on the roof but he heard clamouring and believed they had got off.

He said: "I was not aware they were on the roof when I drove away."

Grantham in the News 1967

Foot and mouth brings farmers to their knees

A tanker is sprayed and has to pass disinfected straw at Caythorpe following the foot and mouth outbreak

AN outbreak of foot and mouth disease hit only a handful of county farms, but restrictions hit everyone.

The agricultural college at Caythorpe Court had its herds worth £25,000 wiped out either by the disease or the preventative slaughter.

There were 120 sheep were infected, but altogether 260 sheep, 236 cattle and 400 pedigree pigs had to be destroyed and burned.

Principal Joe Rowland said: "Two days earlier the students had left for Christmas, but we were isolated. "We were not allowed off."

Sixty cows and 200 breeding ewes were destroyed at Russell Ward's Caythorpe farm. Cattle at Castle Bytham and sheep at nearby Counsthorpe were also victims.

David and Christine Larby called the vet to their pet cow Annie which seemed off colour. When the vet arrived, several blisters had appeared in its mouth and an outbreak of foot and mouth was confirmed.

Their 39-cow herd was destroyed together with a neighbour's 41 sheep. Lincolnshire NFU secretary, Roy Chapman, said: "Every farm had disinfected straw mats. "I got through a lot of rotted wellies.

"It was very, very bad. No one should go through that twice in a lifetime." But farmers did allow football fans to enjoy their FA Cup match against Altrincham.

Fans walked through a disinfectant straw bath to enter the London Road ground to see the match which Grantham lost 3-0.

Into the shadow

GRANTHAM-born Finchley MP Margaret Thatcher, 41, was appointed to the Shadow Cabinet by Tory leader Edward Heath. Before that, she was assistant to shadow chancellor Iain Macleod.

Standard laid up

THE standard of the Machine Gun Corps, which trained at Harrowby and Belton camps in the First World War, was laid up in St Wulfram's Church. The Duke and Duchess of Gloucester and Field Marshal Harding were at the service.

Town fails to 'old 'em

THE end of an FA Cup run for Grantham FC produced another club record.

Beaten 4-0 by Third Division Oldham Athletic in the second round proper, there was a record 6,394 spectators yielding gate receipts of £1,522.70.

Call for more time

GRANTHAM Chamber of Trade called for extra street parking time.

It said the 20-minute wait was not enough for shopping.

Members asked the town council to think again as the short stay was costing them trade.

Get rid of your pram village postman is told

VILLAGE postman Tommy Gibson had to find a new way of carrying letters and parcels on his round after Post Office bosses banned him from using his baby's pram.

Tommy, of Great Gonerby, was told to get rid of the pram after parish council chairman J N G Troughton said he should be supplied with a 'regulation vehicle'.

The 58-year-old had used the pram since taking over the round the previous year.

He said: "For 20 years before that, the village had a post lady who used the pram. I inherited it."

Mr Troughton said: "I admit it was unorthodox. He will be advised it is not included in regulations covering conveyances."

Brewing comes to an end in Grantham

LINKS with brewing in Grantham came to an end after 139 years when Whitbread-owned Flowers Brewery closed its Commercial Road depot.

Thirty-six employers were either made redundant or were found other work within the company.

Founded in 1828 as Mowbray's Brewery, it was taken over by Green's in 1952 which in turn became Flowers in 1954 when brewing ceased. Grantham became a distribution depot. Work was transferred to Loughborough and Stratford-on-Avon.

Carnage on line as trains hit sheep

DOZENS of sheep were killed or later destroyed when trains ran into them on the bridge over the River Witham at Claypole.

The driver of the London to Edinburgh express spotted a flock on the line at the last minute in the morning mist.

He jammed on the brakes but was too late. Other sheep scampered out of the way – into the path of a southbound train.

Farmer D F Allen of Osterfen Lane, Claypole, said afterwards: "It was a heartbreaking sight."

Motor dealer gets a lift from local industry

SEVERAL Grantham companies came together to herald the new era for a local motor dealer.

The Triumph Herald was hoisted on to the roof of North Road Garages, on London Road, opposite the entrance to the football ground.

The crane was supplied by British Crane and Excavator of Dysart Road and the slings to cradle the car by Barrett Packaging of Alma Park. Traffic was reduced to one way during the operation, directed by NRG employees and local police.

GRANTHAM CO-OPERATIVE SOCIETY
LADIES' AND CHILDREN'S DEPARTMENTS

School for demolition

EDUCATION chiefs said Alma Park School, which closed in 1966, was to be demolished.

Vandals had wrecked the premises making it unit for further use. The land was to be developed for housing.

Sleeping on it

OPERATIONS at Grantham Hospital were postponed for a day due to a lack of qualified anaesthetists. Further disruption was expected.

Old shells found

FRAGMENTS of shells millions of years old were discovered at Gorse Farm, Brandon. They were ammonites dating from the end of the Cretaceous period.

Cinema seeks full house

CHURCHMEN objected to Granada's proposals to introduce bingo to the town's only cinema.

Canon Graham Sansbury and the Rev J. Ewart were outraged by the Granada manager's claim that "the majority of Grantham people seem to be gambling fanatics."

Pubs landlords are hit by the new breath test law

THE introduction of the breathalyser was hitting trade at local pubs according to the publicans. They claimed business was down by a third since breath-testing was brought in to cut down drink-driving by Transport Minister Barbara Castle. Royal Queen landlord G E Wheeler said: "People will not walk if it is raining.

"The very bad rainstorm on Tuesday kept people away. The pub was empty."

Six out of 10 licensees reported an increase in off-sales although nothing like enough to cover the loss of bar sales. A police spokesman said: "We have not yet had any cause to ask motorists to take a breathalyser test."

Beam wrecks bridge

A LORRY carrying a 22m-long concrete beam crashed into a house on Bridge End Road, close to the river bridge.

Fortunately, the couple who lived there were about to move and were given the key to their new home a few days early.

The bridge was also badly damaged.

Police relieve boy of bomb

A PUPIL at the Blessed Hugh More School was was excused punishment when the head was told he had been detained by police.

The youngster produced a note from an officer saying "received from Christopher Greensmith of Great Ponton – one article similar in shape to a bomb."

Pc David Rosier had spotted him walking along St Peter's Hill, Grantham, with a metallic object under his arm, shaped like a shell.

He had found it in a sandpit near his home and took it to school to show his friends.

Buzz off

A BEE that flew into the cab of a 10-tonne lorry cause mayhem for the driver.

As he tried to waft it away, he ran off the road into a cornfield, spilling his load of manhole covers and fruit squash. No one was injured.

Move to save George

A MOVE to put a preservation order on the George Hotel was approved by Kesteven County Council.

The resolution was to prevent changes to the Georgian building by redevelopment schemes.

Dovecote goes

THE old dovecote at Hanbeck Farm, Wilsford, was pulled down.

The building, several hundred years old, was in a dangerous state.

It once formed part of a monastic house which was founded in the reign of King Stephen by Hugh de Evermue.

Had your chips

PLANS for a fish and chip shop in Wharf Road were rejected by the borough council.

They said it would be detrimental to the amenities of the locality.

Ring road approved

THE first stage of Grantham's long-awaited inner ring road was approved by Transport Minister Barbara Castle.

It covered 800 metres from Harlaxton Road to Barrowby Road.

The cost of a complete ring road to take east-west traffic from the town was estimated at £280,000.

County surveyor J W Melrose said the work should take six months.

New school opens

GRANTHAM'S Roman Catholic secondary school dedicated to Hugh More who was born in Grantham and died a martyr was opened off Tennyson Avenue.

Off the rails

THE old signalbox at Wilsford level crossing was demolished as part of the British Rail modernisation plan.

Short circuit

A SHORT circuit in a boy's model racing car kit caused a house fire in Croft Drive.

His bed caught fire but it was extinguished by his father with a garden hose.

Scratching shed comes down

WORK began on the £3,000 covered terracing down the side of London Road football ground with the dismantling of the old 'scratching shed' (above), a low structure with crude earth terracing and an odour of its own. The timbers, despite their age, were found to be in excellent condition, but its replacement with a cantilever roof was far more light and airy.

In the background is Harrow Street, its houses also on borrowed time.

Maiden bowls out the camp cricketers

CRICKETERS at RAF Spitalgate turned up their noses when Cpl Jenny Dale asked for a game.

They told her she could umpire, as long as she knew the rules.

But in the station's fixture against the RAF Association of Spalding, Spitalgate were a player short and invited her to take part.

Not only did Jenny (23) top-score in both innings, she took four wickets in eight balls without conceding a run, including the scalp of Spalding's ace batsman.

It was then she let her red-faced team-mates into her secret.

She began playing when she was 11 and was a former member of the Yorkshire junior ladies team and Buckinghamshire Ladies.

Bulldozers move in as occupier eats his lunch

FREDERICK Greensmith was eating his lunch at home, when he heard what sounded like a tank coming up the village lane.

He went outside to investigate, and saw a bulldozer ripping down the semi-detached house next door leaving a gaping hole in his own house. Neighbours were dumbfounded as the owner gave instructions to the driver to raze the unnoccupied cottage, in Fulbeck.

Mr Greensmith, 54. a £9-a-week cleaner at RAF Cranwell, said the owner had been threatening to demolish both Sudthorpe Hill cottages for several months. He had lived there all of his life, and said although the property was dangerous, he had nowhere else to live.

Grantham in the News 1968

Schoolgirls win the day following sports strike

MORE than 100 banner-waving schoolgirls on to St Peter's Hill Green demanded their headmistress changed her mind over sports.

They were protesting over Nina Hewitt's action in withdrawing the newly-opened Walton Girls' School, from the Kesteven Schools' Sports Association. Miss Hewitt said her decision to stop competing against other schools was purely on economic grounds.

She said the girls thought the protest was a "bit of a lark" and blamed outsiders for influencing their actions.

The mini-skirted youngsters said the protest was the latest in a series of moves following a series of sit-down strikes on the playing-field of the Kitty Briggs Lane school.

The head backed down and the school rejoined the association.

Good Friday is bad for trade says rector

RECTOR of Grantham Canon Graham Sansbury was joined by other clergymen in condemning the town's Chamber of Trade following its decision to recommend members to open for the first time on Good Friday.

He said: "We are wholly opposed to this step.

"The small trader is giving in to the multiples. I am very surprised that dress shops and their like are seeing fit to open. Good Friday has been won as a holiday so the people may attend their religious duties that day.

"We are asking bosses to close for a three-hour lunch to allow staff to attend the three-hour service. We will understand and not mind at all if they come to church in their working clothes."

A Chamber of Trade spokesman said: "We have little choice but to follow the multiples which will open Good Friday and close on Monday and Tuesday."

Bridge over the Great North Road

A FOOTBRIDGE was built over the A1 to link southbound customers with the Road House cafe, Stoke Rochford. The prefabricated steel structure was lifted into place by crane.

Horror as airliner bursts into flames

GRANTHAM-born Dorothy Collitt and her husband were among the passengers on a Boeing 707 which crashed at Heathrow Airport.

Seconds after take-off, pilot Capt Charles Taylor spotted his fire warning light was on and nursed the four-engined jet in a wide circle before making an emergency landing.

Seconds later the plane burst into flames.

Her sister, Esther Holt, who still lived in the town, said: "Dorothy tried to climb out of the plane after her husband, but there was an explosion and she had to go back inside.

"However, she got out through an escape hatch."

Mrs Collitt (56), daughter of the late London Road butcher Robert Bell, received only minor cuts and bruises but her husband had multiple fractures. The couple lived in Stockton-on-Tees.

New Harrowby church opens

THE Church of the Ascension, Harrowby, became the first Grantham church to open since St Anne's nearly 60 years earlier. The octagonal shaped building was an extension to the dual purpose church/church hall built a year earlier. The £10,900 project was dedicated by Bishop of Lincoln, the Rt Rev Kenneth Riches.

Barford goes Leyland

LEYLAND Motor Company took over the shares of Grantham firm Aveling Barford.

A spokesman for the new holding company said it would make little difference to the firm's employees.

Bishop in row

A RECTOR described a consecration ceremony by the Bishop of Grantham, the Rt Rev Ross Hook, as "mumbo jumbo".

Rector of Waddington, Gervase Babington, said the ceremony at the village cemetery was "badly out of touch" and "in need of updating."

Lots of reading

A TOTAL of 5,600 books were bought for Grantham Public Library and 2,159 withdrawn.

Jumped to safety

TWO farmhands jumped to safety when fire broke out in a six-bay dutch barn at Swinstead.

Bill Smith and Sid Sentence leapt four metres with the fire at their backs at Frank Eades' farm.

No room for the arts

BOROUGH councillors confirmed they had scrapped plans to build arts centre in Watergate. They told Grantham and District Arts Association they would consider its application to turn Rugby Cottages into an arts centre, but could offer no cash towards the scheme.

Alexander the great

GRANTHAM centre forward for the past five seasons Mike Alexander, was sold to Boston United for £2,000. The club bought him from Gainsborough Trinity for £300.

Light relief

THE proposed inner relief road would only be single carriageway Kesteven County Council said. The second stage, from Harlaxton Road to London Road would also be single. The plan to build a bridge to link Manthorpe and Gonerby Hill Foot was dropped.

New town clerk

KENNETH Russell Cann, deputy town clerk since 1963, became Grantham's youngest town clerk following the retirement of John F Guile.

Norwich-born Mr Cann (30) came to Grantham in 1960 as an articled clerk.

Hospital hit by flu bug

A FLU epidemic laid low the staff at Grantham Hospital forcing bosses to admit emergency cases only. Between 50 and 70 staff were off work suffering from the bug or away on training courses. Other hospitals in the region were also hard hit, leaving no stand-ins available.

All sections were affected including nurses and orderlies. Others were seconded to Leicester Royal Infirmary where they were given special training.

The Co-op dairy was also hit with eight milkmen off the road.

At Barpak, 10 per cent of the staff were off sick, with similar figures reported at other factories.

Wonder diesel engine

BRITISH Leyland's recently launched wonder V8 diesel engine had been designed six years earlier by Grantham man Keith Roberts, grandson of former Richard Hornsby managing director David Roberts.

He developed the engine at the AEC works, Southall, Middlesex.

Gales blast the town

GALE force winds which tore through town brought bricks from a gable end in Albion Place, crashing into the street below.

Occupier Mrs F M Dowlman said: "If someone had been walking past they would have been killed.

"It was very dangerous."

The furious wind also overturned a car travelling along the Grantham bypass. No-one was injured in either accident.

Trees were uprooted in country roads and council workmen were called to clear up the debris. Town dustmen had major problems trying to tidy up on Saturday after paper and boxes from the market were blown along the town centre.

Brian backs Cliff

GRANTHAM musician Brian "Licorice" Locking, rejoined Cliff Richard's backing group The Shadows four years after quitting showbiz to become a Jehovah's Witness.

He returned after his replacement on bass John Rostill (24) collapsed with a nervous breakdown. Brian stood in for three weeks for an engagement at the Talk of the Town in London's West End.

Brian (30) first joined the group in 1962 and was in the film Summer Holiday. He was a founder-member of Grantham's Vagabonds skiffle group.

Greenfingered Alan

FOURTEEN-yearold Alan Lidierth took over the worst twitch-covered allotment on Princess Drive and in 14 months turned into a showpiece garden. Alan, of Belmont Grove, was believed to be the youngest allotment holder in the country.

On top of that, he found time to look after a three-acre garden for a middle-aged couple.

Dog collar is no choke

TRADITIONAL clerical costume was in urgent need of updating, according to Bottesford rector the Rev William Metcalfe.

Writing in his parish magazine The Cross and the Stocks, he said whenever reforms come along, updating the clerical dress scarcely gets a mention. He said: "The dog collar is a large barrier between the parson and the people. "There is no surer way of having a railway compartment to oneself. "The dog collar is uncomfortable, a hard band of steel in chilly weather and a clammy choker on a hot day."

Floods at Billingborough

Drought year turns to floods

THE heaviest July rainfall since 1932 removed threats of a water crisis in Grantham. Although it was cold comfort for holiday makers, it proved to be a godsend for water engineers. The first three months of 1968 were 6cm down on average and Kesteven Water Board was forced to draw on its reserves.

But when 11cm fell in July, rains were 6cm up on average.

Chief engineer Ian Smith said: "We were in the cart up until then.

"We couldn't have hoped for anything better." By November, the Grantham area was suffering the worst floods for half-a-century. Kesteven Fire Service was called out 54 times in 30 hours. Grantham escaped the worst, although the bypass was a metre under water in places.

Billingborough villagers had to move about in boats as up to 50cm of water flooded their homes.

The River Glen overflowed at Corby Glen, closing the main road for several days.

Trapped in van

A NOTTINGHAM van driver was given painkilling injections by Dr Peter Maxted as police hacked at tangled wreckage to free him.

It happened when a lorry jack-knifed under Barrowby Road railway bridge, colliding with his van.

He was taken to Grantham Hospital where he was treated for leg injuries.

Pay to park

THE borough treasurer was told by town councillors to explore the feasibility of charging motorists to park in Guildhall Street and Welham Street car parks.

Holiday ruined

A GLASGOW family who parked their car while they stayed overnight at a Grantham hotel, returned to find all of their clothes and camping gear stolen.

Bypass operating

BARRIERS on the 4km Long Bennington bypass were pulled back by workmen and the newest stretch of the A1 trunk road was opened without ceremony, just after midday. Meanwhile, the Ministry of Transport agreed work on the Leadenham bypass could begin, taking a route north of the village.

New classrooms for Kings School

THE timber building known as the Hut, which had served as classrooms including the art department, at the King's School, Brook Street, since 1918, was finally demolished. It made way for a new three storey extension costing £100,000.

Yellow peril strikes

MARSTON was covered in a yellow haze as sandy soil from surrounding farmland was whipped up by 60mph winds.

Lush lawns in the village overnight became like a scene from the musical Desert Song. The dust caused damage put at hundreds of pounds. It was also a menace to motorists who found themselves unable to see in the thick haze and became bogged down in sand drifts.

Children at Thorold Charity School were sent home by headmaster Brian Vaughan. The air in the classroom became so thick with sand and dust, the children found difficulty in breathing.

School ceiling collapses

THE ceiling of a classroom at Gonerby Hill Foot School fell an hour before 100 pupils were due to take their places.

It was caused by the weight of snow on the roof.

Grantham in the News 1969

Tenants demand action

COUNCIL house tenants in South Witham who had suffered eight years of flooding and the threat of electrocution, formed a militant action group.

They said the council has refused to listen to their complaints.

A spokesman said snow piled up in their lofts and melted, pouring into the bedrooms. They had to sleep with buckets by their beds.

He said: "We pay £3.30 a week for this. The water ruins curtains and carpets."

Theatre's gone, by George

THE George Theatre, home of Grantham Dramatic Society for 15 years, was demolished.

The decision was taken by lease holders Mansfield Breweries.

Secretary Tony Olive said the news was not a shock as they had been expecting it for a year. He said it will not mean the end of the society as it would soon find new premises. It was the group's third move since leaving the Empire Theatre in the 1950s.

Miner killed

A 24-year-old miner was killed at the open-cast Gunby Warren iron ore mine. Gordon Vause was helping to erect a face-shovel when a seven-tonne casting fell on him. He died of head injuries on the way to Grantham Hospital.

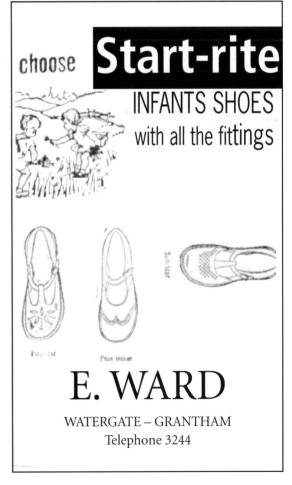

Mystery blaze at teachers' college

A MYSTERY blaze which ravaged part of Kesteven College of Education, Stoke Rochford, was impossible to evaluate according to the county architect's department. Following intensive investigations including forensic tests, police experts said it was arson.

More than 60 firefighters fought the blaze for over four hours as it raged through the art, science and canteen departments, destroying much of the three-storey building.

It was first spotted in the early morning by boilerman Les Watson who saw flames billowing through the roof near the boiler house. Kesteven Fire Brigade was quickly on the scene with crews from Grantham, Bourne, Stamford, Brant Broughton, Corby Glen and Metheringham. They had to brave 15-metre flames and falling burning timbers. Stoke Rochford's chief engineer Jack Bond said: "Roofs were falling in and flames were everywhere. "Fortunately, the fire didn't reach the main building otherwise it would have spread at an alarming rate."

Barracks to be arts centre

NEWS that the former barracks on Sandon Road would be turned into an arts centre was welcomed by Grantham Arts Association.

Kesteven County Council agreed the scheme which had attracted a £30,000 grant from the Arts Council.

Cost of decorating and alterations were put at £22,000, constructing an auditorium £43,000, backstage facilities £19,000 plus a further £7,000 for a car park.

Secretary of Grantham Arts, Tony Olive said: "We could have it going within months."

Must pay to park

MOTORISTS had to dip into their pockets to park their cars for the first time.

Council workmen put bollards around the Greenwoods Row car park, leaving only one entrance with a pay kiosk. It also had a height restriction board.

Parkers had to pay in Welham Street car park too, where a pay box was also installed.

Shoppers had to pay 5p for up to two hours and 10p for longer.

Had its chips

AN application to convert Fashion Fayre, 29A High Street, into a fish and chip shop was turned down by Grantham Borough Council. A corporation spokesman said: "It would be detrimental to the amenities of the locality."

Rates up

GRANTHAM Building Society announced an increase in the borrowing rate from 7.625 per cent to 8.5 per cent.

Mason's last

THE Mason's Arms, Sudbrook, closed after 130 years. Regulars complained if they had been given more notice they could have protested at its loss.

Hot recording

JANE Birkin, daughter of Grantham-born film star Judy Campbell, hit the Top 20 charts but her record was banned by the BBC.

Originally penned for Brigitte Bardot, J'taime moi non plus, which she sang with her husband French star Serge Gainsbourg, was regarded too risqué by the corporation.

New Post Office opens

THE new General Post Office opened on St Peter's Hill in 1969, using the standard 'house style'.

A feature of the building was the retention of holly trees.

The GPO said it planned to install outdoor seating in the area.

The Post Office had been in the Market Place until 1922, when it moved to St Peter's Hill. The building on the corner of Wharf Road had yet to be demolished to make way for the new sorting office and van park.

The old sorting office, a former Army hut, had been there since 1917.

This replacement was no larger but the layout was far superior.

The original one was then pulled down and a new entrance to the sorting office opened on Wharf Road.

School pools overtake Quin memorial

MUCH of the enthusiasm which carried Grantham Quincentenary indoor swimming pool plan forward had disappeared.

The scheme – the cost of which had risen to £194,000 and was yet to be started – at least got a small boost for an unlikely source.

Visitors from all over the world at Vacu-Lug Tyre Organisation's forum at the firm's Gonerby Hill Foot base, passed the hat round at the closing dinner. They raised £176 for the swimming pool funds and a further £37 for War on Want. In the meantime, the King's School and the National School opened their own swimming pools.

The King's was an indoor version while the National School installed a gas-heated outdoor pool, 12m by 8m. It cost £2,000.

National School

King's School

Mile of money

CHILDREN laid 4,800 pennies along Princess Drive, Harrowby Lane and Edinburgh Road to raise funds for the Church of the Ascension.

While the coppers measured almost a mile from end to end, the value amounted to only £20.

End of the line for quarry loco

THE days of the steam engine came to the end of the line at Harlaxton quarry. The locomotives which had served Denton, Woolsthorpe and Harlaxton quarries since 1941 were either scrapped or sold, as diesel engines took over the work.

Driver Anthony Bass, of Denton, said: "I'm quite happy with the change to oil. Diesel is a lot cleaner." Owners Stewart and Lloyd Minerals said Salmon, Belvoir, Rhondda and Ajax were sold to collectors but Achilles, Grantham, Rutland and Denton were scrapped.

Biggest bullock too big

HERBERT the biggest bullock in the world, was denied his place at Grantham's Mid-Lent Fair – because he was too big.

The trouble was, he needed lots of space and that's one thing the town centre site was short of.

Market superintendent T C Coates said: "There just wasn't enough room to squeeze in his tent. Westgate is too narrow at the best of times."

High risk of electric fires

CORONER John Pert warned against the dangers of open electric fires. It followed the death of Ethel May Bellamy, who slipped on a carpet. He returned a verdict of accidental death on Miss Bellamy, of Billingborough.

Her sister Ada said her sister's nightdress had caught fire.

Mr Pert said: "I doubt the wisdom of using this type of heating in a bedroom."

Bridge End Road maltings crash

ANOTHER old Grantham building made way to the future as a former maltings fell to the bulldozers.

The Lee and Grinling-owned building, on Bridge End Road, was built at the start of the 19th Century and at one time belonged to Joe Thompson, of Harrowby Road.

It was sold to Lee and Grinling in 1930.

The site was developed by Gainsborough Petroleum as a 24-hour self-service filling station, run by Grantham Motor Company.

Spare a copper

LINCOLNSHIRE Constabulary was looking for men aged 19-29 and at least 1.73m tall to join the force. Pay was £1,270 per year plus free housing for married men. Applications were also invited for police cadets aged 16 to 18 which carried a salary of £390 to £470 per year.

Cold reception

CHRISTIAN Salvesen opened a cold store at Easton, near Colsterworth, capable of storing 8,000 tonnes of frozen products.

No Place to play

THE rural district council agreed to install security fencing following complaints from Fulbeck parish council that children play inside the village's sewage disposal works.

Store fire

WALLWORKS carpet and bedding store, Castlegate, was badly damaged by fire John Wallwork and his son Stephen, discovered the blaze and fought it with extinguishers. It was spotted by Stephen who lived in a flat opposite.

The shell was undamaged but stock damage was put at £19,000.

1970 Grantham in the News

Bus hits coal cart

FOUR coach passengers were taken to hospital following a collision with a coal lorry under Springfield Road bridge.

Neither coalmen in the lorry owned by O C Storey was injured and the passengers were not detained.

Coroner kept busy

A RECORD number of deaths were reported to the coroner. John Pert said he dealt with 88 deaths in 1969, 23 more than the previous year.

He said: "This is the highest in my 17 years as coroner.

"It's a very gloomy record."

There were 51 males and 27 females.

Tunnel vision

THE pedestrian tunnel between Huntingtower Road and Station Road was closed for repairs for the first time since it was built in 1850.

A 12cm concrete lining was built inside to give extra strength for the high-speed trains passing over it at 95mph.

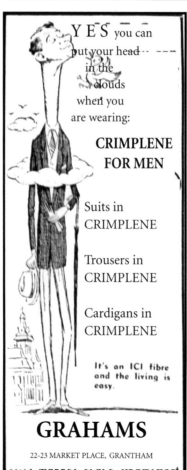

YES you can put your head in the clouds when you are wearing:

CRIMPLENE FOR MEN

Suits in CRIMPLENE

Trousers in CRIMPLENE

Cardigans in CRIMPLENE

It's an ICI fibre and the living is easy.

GRAHAMS

22-23 MARKET PLACE, GRANTHAM

Road roller rolls over

ONCE again the area suffered heavy snowfalls. Conditions on Somerby Hill were treacherous in February.

A pneumatic roller made by Aveling Barford toppled over and slid down the hill during a snowstorm. No one was injured

Move fair plea by traders

THE centuries old Mid-Lent Fair came under fire from Westgate traders. Businesses on the east side of Westgate said they were fed up of the stalls always being on their side of the street.

They called on town clerk Russell Cann to alternate it in future years.

Market superintendent T C Coates said it had been put on the east side because the curvature of the road gave more footage on the east.

New vicar 'sold' brown bread

A TOP TV ad-man became the new vicar of St Anne's Church, Grantham.

The Rev Norton Harvey Collard was also involved in the theatre. He acted, produced and wrote for the Erith Theatre Guild for 14 years. He also wrote several plays, reviews and lyrics for musicals. Mr Collard, 48, was in advertising for 20 years before his ordination.

In the latter years he concentrated on TV advertising and was responsible for several campaigns for major clients including the slogan 'Don't say brown, say Hovis'.

Flying Scotsman makes its debut in the park

GRANTHAM'S miniature Flying Scotsman went into service in a field next to Wyndham Park.

Leslie Broadbridge, who moved to Grantham some 18 months ago, had built the locomotive with his friend George Bolton 20 years earlier.

Mr Broadbridge contacted the council which allowed him to lay tracks in the field next to Manthorpe Road.

It cost 4p a ride for children, at weekends and bank holidays. There were three coaches and planned to add another two.

At last! Conservatives open doors to the ladies

THE 100-year-old Grantham Conservative Club sounded the last post on its men only tradition.

The sex-bar was lifted following the opening of the £22,000 extension to the Middlemore Yard premises by Sir Donald Kaberry.

Chairman-secretary Jack Barnes said: "It is a matter of progress.

"At first there was opposition to women being allowed in, but at the third attempt it went through.

"It was a great step forward.

"We have had 150 new applications for membership, 120 of them women."

He said: "This is merely the provision of a pleasant place where you can take your lady."

At the opening ceremony, Mr Barnes told the lady members: "Our gentlemen members have been instructed in the correct thing to say when they miss the jackpot or someone knocks over their beer."

The club was originally looking to build new premises but settled for extending its present one.

Dustbin ban

THE collection of refuse in dustbins was condemned as outdated by Grantham's chief public health inspector Mr C. Taylor.

He said they should be replaced by paper sacks or other containers.

Spitfire on the green

A WARTIME Spitfire appeared in front of the Guildhall, St Peter's Hill. But it hadn't crash-landed. It was a promotion for the film Battle of Britain being shown at the Granada cinema.

Scotland Yard probes manor painting theft

A MAN posing as a priest made off with a 16th Century painting worth £2,000 from Harlaxton Manor.

The man twice entered the manor claiming first to be Father Cantry, then Father Preston.

The painting, St George in his study by Marius Van Romersale (1497-1567), hung near the main entrance.

It showed the head and shoulders of a man reading from an open bible written in Hebrew.

The painting, in a black and gilt frame, measured 100cm x 130cm. It was owned by the Roman Catholic Purposes.

The theft was discovered by gamekeeper Mr J Foster.

Det Insp Charles Mawer of New Scotland Yard, was put in charge of the investigation.

Harlaxton Manor, owned by the Jesuit Order, was formerly a campus for Stanford University, California.

Town centre conservation

A LARGE part of Grantham town centre became a conservation area under the Civic Amenities Act.

The object was to retain areas with special architectural or historic interest by preserving and enhancing the character of defined areas. The oldest area included St Wulfram's Church, King's School, Grantham House, and National Trust land either side of the River Witham.

The Market Place and Westgate with their fine continuity of Georgian buildings were also included together with St Peter's Hill, Manthorpe Road, Vine Street and Castlegate.

Girl attacked on way home from dance

A SIXTEEN-year-old girl was brutally attacked on the way home from a dance at Bmarco social club, Springfield Road.

She was walking alone along Harlaxton Road when she was seriously assaulted.

A young man dragged into a field next to Grantham Electrical Engineering.

Her attacker fled towards Springfield Road and she made her way back to her Earlesfield home, from where her parents called police. Police searched the area and conducted house-to-house inquiries.

Back to the ice age

THE Premier Rinks were exposed when builders merchants English Bros (later Jewsons) brought in the demolition men to their Wharf Road depot in 1970.

The building was originally Richard John Boyall's carriage and pram works, later becoming the orderly room for the 2nd Battalion Lincolnshire Regiment.

By the 1880s it was the Premier Skating Rink and later doubled up as the King's Picture Hall, a cinema seating 800.

In 1918 it was home to the YMCA and local dramatic societies before returning to commercial use.

Lead theft from roof

DARING burglars stole 500kg of lead worth £100 from the roof of the South China Restaurant, London Road.

It was discovered by agents of the owner Chun Che Lo after the interior was swimming with water following heavy rain.

A CID spokesman said: "Thieves took a big risk. They could have easily slipped and broken their necks."

TV star booked

EGBERT Nosh, a character devised by Barrowby children's author Paul Groves, was turned into a colourful picture book. Cartoon films of his exploits were produced in colour for BBC1. Mr Groves was head of English at St Hugh's School, Grantham.

Fewer fillings

A QUANTITY of amalgam – metal used for teeth fillings – was stolen from dentists Miller and Braunton, of Church Trees.

Pay to spray

GARDENERS who used their sprinklers to water their lawns had to pay the price when Kesteven Water Board introduced a £3 a year charge for continuous irrigation schemes. There was no charge for hand-held hoses.

Town in Cup thriller

GRANTHAM FC manager Terry Bly claimed his first Football League scalp when his team beat Stockport County 2-1 in the first round of the FA Cup. But the home fans also witnessed the ugly side of football against the Fourth Division side, with chants of "A-g-g-r-o aggros", fighting, pitch invasions and a stabbing.

Missing, by George

THE George Hotel was omitted from the AA handbook after several decades. The previous year it had a three-star billing. Regional controller Michael Rose said: "If a hotel does not apply or does not meet our minimum standards, it will not be included."

Chime of the times

THE clock of St Wulfram's Church went on strike after the 1.5m pendulum fell off.

Bmarco taken over

THE future of Bmarco was assured after Swiss company Oerlikon-Buhrle took over the assets of Hispano Suiza, which included the Springfield Road factory.

Lion Saved

A PETITION signed by 86 villagers caused brewers Watney Mann to give the Red Lion, Caythorpe, a reprieve from planned closure. It dated from 1650.

Mint condition

JOHN Lee and Son won a contract from the Royal Mint to supply 1.2million sacks required to bag the new decimal coins.

Ex-alderman remembered

EDUCATION Secretary Margaret Thatcher returned home for the dedication of a lectern to her father's memory, at Finkin Street Methodist Church.

Former Alderman Alfred Roberts had died in February.

He served on the town council for a quarter of a century and was a lay preacher.

It was paid for through donations, including a contribution from the Grantham Rotary Club.

The first to read from the lectern, in Finkin Street Methodist Church, was Rotarian and toyshop owner Allan Arbon.

Pictured with Mrs Thatcher are her sister Muriel Cullen, his widow and ministers the Rev Bailey and the Rev Cox.

Tossing good time

THE second annual Pancake Races were held in Wide Westgate, before huge crowds. Grantham was pushed into second place by Boston, with Ilkeston and Spalding also taking part.

Grantham in the News 1971

Supermarket plan for Hornsby site rejected

The former Hornsby foundry and other workshops on London Road.

THE 11-acre London Road site which until three years ago housed Alfred Wiseman and Co was set to be sold, creating hundreds of jobs.

A bid of £100,000-plus was being put together by a consortium of local businessmen. Accountant John Hindmarch said: "We are putting a substantial sum of money into this venture as well as into the development of the site.

"We see this as a viable proposition.

"We do not see ourselves as fairy godmothers but it will benefit us and benefit the town."

The takeover followed the planning refusal for a supermarket on the site, first developed by Richard Hornsby in the 1830s. Asda had hoped to build a 4,600 sq m American style superstore on the site. Opposing consent, Coun John Wallwork said: "Nothing is going to be cheaper and there will be no better service than already available on High Street.

Parents fined for boys' acts

THE parents of two boys who went on a wrecking spree at a local football club's changing huts, were each fined £2 by magistrates.

The boys aged 11 and 12 broke into the property belonging to Earlesfield Rangers causing damge put at £10. They caused damage to the walls, floor and doors as well as smashing windows.

About 200 plastic cups were damaged by being jumped on.

The parents said it was more mischief than malicious and the boys had been led on.

Mayor dies in office

MAYOR of Grantham Norman Bee, died on his way to work.

Mr Bee, 59, a cost clerk at Industrial Engine (Sales), London Road, was taken to hospital where he died.

A member of the Salvation Army, Mr Bee was born in Stamford Street and educated at the Boys' Central School.

Yanks move into manor

EIGHTY-five students from Evansville University, Indiana, arrived at Harlaxton Manor. They were the first contingent following the faculty's takeover of the lease from Californian-based Stanford University. There were five tutors on the payroll. The Gothic-style manor was owned by the Jesuit Order, which they bought from Mrs Violet van der Elst.

Old folk badgered

THE Co-op, St Catherine's Road, was accused of badgering pensioners to take more milk than they needed.

It followed a move to sell milk checks in batches of five instead of singly.

Customer Evelyn Hickman said: "Next thing you know they'll be selling tea in pound (½kg) bags."

Walter Thacker of Greater Nottingham Co-op said it was to streamline queues by cutting waiting times.

Going off pop

A HAND grenade was discovered by workmen clearing an outhouse behind the Blue Lion pub, Market Place.

Finally opened

AFTER a seven-year wait, Grantham indoor swimming pool finally opened.

The £114,450 pool in Union Street was opened by Joint Parliamentary Under-Secretary of State Eldon Griffiths. And it proved to be a big hit. In the first six days 2,200 swimmers plus 25 life members of the pool used it.

Manager David Skinners said 400 visitors a day was well above expectations.

"I suppose people wanted to see their new pool, having waited so long."

Children paid 8p admission plus 5p deposit on a locker key.

Vicar's poor salesmanship earns him a brand new car

WHEN the vicar of the Church of the Ascension, Edinburgh Road, failed to sell all of his batch of raffle tickets for League of Friends of Grantham Hospital, he bought all that was left himself.

And it turned out to be good fortune for the Rev Peter Dadd, as one of them took the top prize – a new Ford Capri worth £1,000.

A delighted Mr Dadd said afterwards: "I must have felt a bit generous when I bought the tickets I couldn't sell."

Young criminals guide

CHEEKY youngsters stole guide books from St Wulfram's Church and sold them door-to-door – claiming they were doing so for the organ fund. The vicar, Canon Graham Sansbury, asked confronted householders to call the police.

Town in the red

GRANTHAM FC plunged £1,349 into the red with a loss on the season of £238, despite slashing wages and increased gates. Wages were cut from £6,301 the previous year to £5,978. Gates were up, taking £7,581 (£5,385) but expenses also rose.

Co-op resolution

GRANTHAM Co-operative Society closed down to become a member of the Greater Nottingham Co-operative Society.

Short time for Kontak

THE collapse of aircraft engine maker Rolls Royce led to short time for Kontak Manufacturing, of Londonthorpe Lane.

Thirty-seven employed in the aircraft section were made redundant while 150 of the remaining 200 were put on a three-day week.

Workers strike as more are thrown out of work

EMPLOYMENT and industrial relations hit an all-time low.

There were more than 1,000 out of work in September, 7 per cent of available workforce, nearly double the same month the previous year.

There were also protests against the Government's Industrial Relations Bill.

After meeting in Dysart Park, 130 shop floor workers marched along London Road and through town, ending with a petition being handed over to MP Joe Godber.

On the same day, 1,200 men downed tools at Aveling Barford resulting in a total shutdown.

Kontak's shop stewards reported 95 per cent of members on strike for the day although bosses said only 62 of the 370 workforce were absent.

The Post Office strike dragged on throughout the month, with only 14 of 27 switchboard operators at work. Volunteers and scouts ensured hospital mail got through during the national stoppage.

Peacock cries anger visitors

HARLAXTON villagers were being driven mad by a peacock on the loose.

They were woken early and could only watch as it wandered across their gardens.

Villager John Cragg said: "You can't get near it.

"It roams around gardens and flies about wailing like a dreaded banshee.

"It makes a terrible row early in the morning."

A police spokesman said: "I've never caught a peacock before. It would be very difficult."

Scotland Yard dawn raid traps forgers

A DAWN raid on a Long Bennington farm brought a rich harvest for Scotland Yard

Officers from the Counterfeit Currency Squad swooped on Authorpe Farm, seizing printing equipment and 500 forged £5 notes.

They were supported by Bank of England officials who examined the forgeries.

Police were alerted after the purchase of a Mercedes sports car in Surrey, where £2,850 was paid in notes, which later proved to be fake.

Violence mars Town's FA Trophy victory

A SCUFFLE behind the goal, missiles thrown at Grantham keeper Chris Gardiner and the referee struck in the face by a divot was only the start of crowd trouble at Grantham's FA Challenge Trophy match at Connah's Quay.

Both sets of supporters had minor skirmishes throughout the game which Grantham won 2-1.

As they left the ground, two windows in one of Town's supporters coaches were smashed.

One of the drivers, Kenneth Prince, said: "My vehicle was hit three times, so was the second.

The third had two windows smashed." Organiser of the trip, Alf Cox, said two of the passengers received minor injuries.

Coach owner Cecil Blankley, of Colsterworth, said in future he would ask for police protection.

Butchers raided

NEARLY £350 in cash was stolen in a raid on Watkin and Sons' London Road shop.

There was more cash than usual as they had the new decimal coinage ready for the changeover due to take place the following day, February 15. The theft was discovered by an employee arriving for work.

New Club

GREAT Gonerby, with a population of under 1,000, opened its £30,000 social club which would be the pride of any town or city. The original Great Gonerby Institute had been housed in a former Army hut bought from Belton Camp in 1921.

Steelweld's big order

STEELWELD, of Springfield Road, which 12 months earlier had laid off one-seventh of its workforce, won a major £700,000 order to supply two fully-automated press welding lines to the USSR. During the previous year, the Grantham company also completed the Ford Cortina underbody line.

Cost cuts dinners

THE price of school dinners shot up from 9p to 12p per day, at the start of the summer term. It resulted in a turn-off for parents, with 1,800 meals a day fewer consumed by the Kesteven children.

Calling time

HAROLD and Hilda Dale called time at Westgate pub Frederick Fletcher, after 40 years in the licensed trade working a seven day week. They decided to retire from the pub after 21 years following its takeover by Ansell's Brewery.

Growing up

THE year's census revealed Grantham had a population of 27,913, compared with 25,048 10 years previously and 23,555 in 1951.

All gas and gaiters

GRANTHAM Taxi Company, of Cambridge Street, became the first cab firm to have a liquid petroleum gas-powered taxi.

Proprietor Don Hallam said the Cortina was an experiment and if successful he would also convert his nine Zephyrs.

Double joy for Town

THE town's soccer team was rewarded with a civic reception at the Guildhall, after winning the Midland League Championship and League Cup double.

Deputy Mayor Tom Scott said the footballers were "wonderful ambassadors for Grantham."

Firework fine

A 16-year-old who threw a lighted firework from a train window was fined £3 with a further £2 for giving the guard a false name and address.

Drug pushers on the increase

THE number of names on the county police list of drugs pushers and takers rocketed. The total on their list in 1964 was 65, but it had rocketed to just over 2,000. Pc Barry Davey told a meeting called by Earlesfield Youth Centre: "There is no set answer to the problem of drugs."

He called on parents to talk openly to discourage their children but did not think discussion at school was wise.

No one hurt in bridge strike

A CONTAINER lorry struck Dysart Road private railway bridge, bringing a girder down on to a car.

The vehicle was a write-off but miraculously, no one was hurt.

The bridge originally carried the Ambergate Railway line but in recent years had been a private siding for John Lee & Son.

Grantham in the News 1972

Striker cleared of ref strike

A SPECIAL meeting of the Football Association at the George Hotel, Grantham, cleared Grantham striker Bob Norris of striking a referee. In a statement afterwards, the commission said although they accepted referee Atkin was punched in the back during a match against Boston United, there was no proof Norris was the culprit.

Token bid

THE borough council agreed that a limited number of boat people, fleeing persecution in the Far East, would be found houses in Grantham.

Top trade unionist backs jobless rally

ABOUT 80 people including women and children, marched through Grantham protesting against high unemployment.

The march, organised by Grantham Trades Council, began in the Market Place, and took in Westgate and Wharf Road on its way to the Guildhall. They carried placards demanding the right to work together with the immediate resignation of Prime Minister Edward Heath and his Conservative Government. At the Guildhall, the meeting was addressed by TUC assistant general secretary Len Murray. He said: "If the unemployed of Britain lined up 10 abreast, the queue would stretch from Grantham to London. "This has to change, even if that means a change of national Government."

Kings and KGGS to become mixed schools

THE King's School and Kesteven and Grantham Girls' School were to become mixed schools going to Grantham College for their sixth-form studies.

That was Kesteven Education Committee's plan for the future of Grantham, already rejected by parents. They had thrown it out by 768 votes to 540.

Director of Education G Ronald Scott said: "By the mid-70s we will need 1,000 more places. We had to take a bold decision."

Pub loos are just not up to scratch

PUB toilets did not come up to a decent standard, according to chief public health inspector J A F Saville. He said too many of them had no indoor loos.

He said: "In this day and age, external, uncorfortable basic facilities are not suitable.

"We have no statutory powers but we are slowly encouraging brewery companies to provide washing facilities. It is a poor reflection that we cannot expect hand-washing facilities in public toilets as a matter of course. It is essential to minimise the spread of gastro-internal infections."

Staff join new firm

WHEN merger talks between John Lee & Son (Grantham) with Blackburn steel giant C Walker & Son fell through, bosses thought it was the end of the line for their employees.

But when Walker's Steel took over a 4.5 hectare site on Spittlegate Level and built a massive warehouse, all of Lee's stockholding staff walked out to join the new firm.

Guildhall is capped

GRANTHAM Guildhall had a new cap fitted above the clock tower. Workmen, including local umpire Vic Heppenstall, worked 30m above street level to carry out the work in gale force winds.

The copy canopy replace one in wrought iron.

Drought

THE Grantham area suffered the worst drought for more than 30 years. Only the new supply from Aswarby ensured water supplies were kept off ration.

Kesteven Water Board chief engineer Ian Smith warned: "The situation is not likely to improve unless we get substantial quantities of rain.

"People are using water they don't really need."

Left back left behind

GRANTHAM FC's victory at Bangor nearly ended in farce when fullback Gerry Taylor was stranded in North Wales.

After sending a telegram he discovered the bus had already left for Colwyn Bay, where a meal had been booked for the team and officials.

He finally arrived by taxi at the end of the soup course.

Factory closes

STEELWELD announced it was closing its Springfield Road factory and going into liquidation.

Founded in 1959, at one time 350 people worked there, but 270 had been released over two years.

At the end, 78 people were made redundant.

Steamed up

PLANS to turn the Wharf Road slipper baths into a steam room or sauna baths were considered by the borough council.

Court on the move

COURT cases were heard at the Guildhall for the last time.

They were to be heard at Spittlegate courthouse, London Road. A second court room together with the offices were furbished at the new venue.

Chairman of the bench since 1949, Dr J H Hopper, said it was a move for the better.

Last post

RESIDENTS in the Springfield Road area were furious. Only weeks after the sub-post office closed, the postbox at the bottom of Stamford Street was sealed up by the GPO.

More houses

THE borough council agreed for a 180-acre housing development to be built between Barrowby Road and Barrowby stream.

Bug Hunt

A SEVERE attack of death watch beetle was discovered in the choir seats at Bitchfield Church during decoration for harvest festival celebrations. They were removed immediately.

Dangerous machinery

SCRAP merchants John Lee and Son was fined £75 by borough magistrates for failing to secure guards on machinery properly. Factory inspector Bryan Hopkinson told magistrates the machines were capable of ripping a man's arm from its socket.

Pigs perish

ABOUT 100 pigs were roasted alive in a £10,000 blaze at Normanton, near Bottesford.

Sticky situation

MOTORISTS found themselves in a mess when a tanker leaked its load of 250 gallons of a thick slippery fluid along Harlaxton Road and Wharf Road.

Four star treatment for Grantham mums

EXPECTANT mums jumped for joy when the new maternity-gynaecology department opened at Grantham Hospital. It meant babies would be born with four-star hotel amenities.

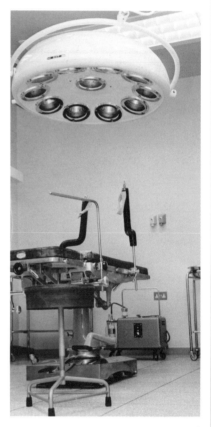

When the three-storey, £440,000 unit was fully operational, Hill View maternity unit, Dysart Road, closed.

Originally, the department was designed to take 48 maternity cases plus 10 cots for special care babies.

But an unpredicted fall in birth-rate caused hospital bosses to cut this to 36 cases.

This made room for 16 beds in the gynaecology unit.

The building included a delivery suite with three single delivery rooms and an operating theatre.

Obstetrician-gynaecologist Mr R. N. Spencer-Gregson was in charge of the new department.

Work starts on new fire station

WORK began on Grantham's new £136,000 fire station. It was built on the site of the previous station on Harlaxton Road.

Personnel moved into temporary buildings once demolition began, while two houses on nearby Denton Avenue were converted into offices.

The old station was erected in 1945 and was planned to be replaced within 10 years. But cash constraints and priorities at other stations put the town station to the back of the queue.

Last year, Kesteven County Council was urged by the Inspector of Fire Services to improve the town's facilities.

Saxon remains found

A TEAM of young archaeologists raced against the clock to unearth the secrets of the Saxons.

They were given only six months to save Saxon artifacts at Loveden Hill, near Hough-on-the-Hill. Aveling Barford lent the group earth-moving equipment to speed up the work on Lord Brownlow's ¾ hectare site. Among the finds was the remains of a warrior, buried with a child and a dog.

Three headless skeletons were found and a 5m Roman pillar was also unearthed.

High Street shut by bingo hall slip

A TEN-metre length of concrete weighing more than a tonne became detached on the roof of the Granada bingo hall.

Only the 'G' sign, projecting from the wall, prevented it from crashing to the ground. Workmen were called to make it safe.

It was shortly after it ceased to be a cinema and became a bingo hall.

The fight to halt the closure of Grantham's last cinema failed, when the Granada showed its final film in April.

The company, which had hinted it may build a smaller cinema, decided to concentrate on bingo.

Town Clerk Antony Jowett said: "The borough council view this with considerable dismay.

"It will deprive people both in the town and living in the surrounding area of a valuable, social amenity, in a place where social amenities are at a premium." Jane Porter (15) handed in a 286-name petition from St Hugh's School.

Staff at Coles Cranes wrote a letter signed by 230 employees "deploring the action".

But it fell on the deaf ears of Granada management, and the final film before full time bingo was the poorly attended Tales of Beatrix Potter.

Car park plan approved

OUTLINE permission for owner Wallwork Properties to demolish Pidcock's malting, Welham Street, was permitted by the council's planning committee. They also passed plans for a multi-storey car park on the site.

Bank on one way

BARCLAYS Bank asked the borough council to make Guildhall Street one-way, closed to traffic from High Street.

The bank's premises were on the corner of the two roads.

Top film

THE Ruling Class, shot at Harlaxton Manor and starring Peter O'Toole, was named as Britain's entry in the Cannes Film Festival. Bugle comes home

Put that light out

TEMPORARY traffic lights were installed at Springfield Road bridge as short-term measure while the borough council decided how to make it safer

Mega rise machinists

AVELING Barford's 220 machine-shop engineers returned to work after a 10-day strike. They had already turned down a £4 increase and a minimum £27.50 per week before accepting the new offer. Both parties refused to disclose the agreed figure.

Road and bridge closed

SPITTLEGATE Hill railway bridge was rebuilt at a cost of £98,000 – a third more than estimated. The road was closed to traffic for six months. Wyville Road was resurfaced to cope with the extra cars.

Bosses sack strikers

FACTORY bosses refused to take back strikers picketing their Alma Park factory. The industrial action was over the sacking of two of their women colleagues at Superfoam.

Managing director Lewis Rosen, said: "One of the women was sacked because she was impossible to work with, the other was made redundant."

The sacking provoked a walkout by nine women.

Management said they had broken their contract of employment by their action. Mr Rosen said since the sackings and the strike, the remaining workforce had increased output.

Grantham in the News 1973

Prince visits King's

PRINCE Philip visited Grantham schools in May to inspect the success of his Duke of Edinburgh Award scheme.

He arrived at St Hugh's Comprehensive School by Wessex helicopter. Following a visit to the King's School, he flew to Melton Mowbray for the next leg of his arduous tour. Planting a tree at the King's School, he quipped: "It will be dead next week."

Tyre fire at Corby

SIX fire crews were called to deal with a blaze among thousands of tyres at a tip at Corby Glen.

"Ghouls go home" say angry villagers

RESIDENTS in Little Humby were infuriated by sightseers who poured into their tiny hamlet.

The ghouls turned up at the tiny backwater, with a population of fewer than 50, to see where a villager had been murdered and a man had died of gun shot wounds by his own hand.

The body of Hungarian-born Mrs Juliana Sophie Jakab (54) was discovered in the bedroom of her spacious cottage by her home help.

She had been violently battered about the head and brutally raped.

Det Supt John Standish, in charge of the investigation, said: "There had been a considerable struggle and there is no doubt she made an attempt to defend herself.

"Had she submitted without a fight I believe she would not have died. "The room was in absolute chaos." Later, a 23-year-man was found dead with gunshot wounds in a nearby house.

Villager Maurice Arden said: "People have been coming in since it happened.

"It was really bad at the weekend, particularly Sunday.

"There was almost a convoy of cars around the village green."

Council pooh-poohs dog poo bin proposals

PLANS to install doggy loos and a pets' exercise area were laughed out of the council chamber.

Ald Lloyd Ramsden said: "I can see any worker who would have to clean up after the dogs being called 'Dan Dan the dog toilets man'. It's ridiculous, a huge joke."

Plans put before councillors showed the site to be on disused allotments behind the indoor swimming pool, Union Street. But councillors told officers to think again. Borough surveyor Harry Haworth agreed the dog toilets idea was not practical but thought the exercise area should go ahead.

He said the experience in other towns was that people couldn't be bothered to go out of their way to use them.

Mr Ramsden said: "Dogs do create a problem but someone has gone too far with this plan."

Night club planned

PLANS to convert Swallow's Mill, Bridge End Road, into a hotel, restaurant and night club were approved by Grantham borough councillors. It was to include a glass dance floor over the river and waterwheel.

Shopping mall for Alma Park?

A MASSIVE out-of-town shopping development was proposed for Alma Park. It would be only the second of its type in the UK, the first being at Cardiff.

Teape-White wanted to build a superstore, nearly double the size of the Fine Fare store, Castlegate. The area would cover 4,700sq m including spaces for 1,000 cars. The complex was to include a filling station.

Douglas finds new role

FORMER King's School pupil Douglas Gorin joined the Bel Canto Singers, resident group at the London Palladium.

Until then, he toured the country with the Black and White Minstrels for several years.

Douglas, of Edward Street, previously worked in the costing office at Aveling Barford for 10 years after leaving school. He was involved in amateur dramatics and worked in singing and dancing as a semi-professional before going full time.

Plans to move town soccer club are shelved

PLANS by Buckminster Trust for a sports stadium, including a new home for Grantham FC, were shelved. The proposal was for land on Springfield Road, currently used as allotments.

Council planners ordered a review of allotments in the town.

Mr A J Potter, of Buckminster Trust Estate, said originally they had wanted to move the town's football club to Spittlegate Level but the club indicated as many supporters went on foot, they wanted to be in town.

Robin Woods for the allotment holders, said most of them wanted to stay there.

He said: "They are on first-class agricultural land and are the right place for residents in the area."

Lorry blocked High Street

A LORRY overturned on Grantham High Street spilling its load of rags, bringing the town centre to a standstill.

Pony invasion was no joke

BUSINESSMAN Doug Bates thought he was having his leg pulled when a friend called to ask about the ponies on his front garden. But returning to his Somerby Hill home, he found it was true. They had escaped from a Little Ponton riding school.

He said: "No problem. It saves cutting the lawn."

Poor instructions by packaging firm

GRANTHAM packaging company Barpak was fined £150 for failing to instruct an employee on how to use a circular saw.

The Alma Park company was fined £150 for contravening the woodworking machinery regulation.

The man was using the saw when a piece of wood flew back and hit his hand, knocking it into the operating saw.

He fractured his hand in four places and injured the tendons of three fingers and a thumb.

He claimed he had never been instructed how to use the saw.

Man trapped in sand

A TWENTY-six year old man was rescued unharmed after spending four hours trapped to his waist by sand in a 10m hopper at C and G Concrete, Grantham.

People rising

A REVISED population of Grantham issued by the Registrar General showed there were 28,030 residents in the town.

Rolled over

GRANTHAM Mayoress Kathleen Porter achieved her lifetime ambition when she drove an Aveling Barford road roller. It was a sad day for the company. She was driving the 5,822nd and final GC medium weight three-wheeler the company had made. Production should have finished in 1965 but was continued due to its popularity.

Police chief dies

CHIEF Supt William Goosey, Grantham Divisional Commander for the past six years, collapsed and died at the annual police ball held at Arnoldfield. He was 55.

He was awarded an MBE in the 1972 birthday honours and served in the force for 34 years.

Going bananas

THE Banana Box, a play by Grantham author and former Boys' Central School pupil Eric Chappell, received good reviews from critics who watched it at the Apollo Theatre, London.

Raid at the manor

SCOTLAND Yard's fine arts squad was called in to investigate a break-in at Denton Manor.

Rooms were ransacked and 81 items of jewellery and porcelain worth £17,750 were stolen.

Sir Oliver and Lady Welby were away at the time and the burglary was discovered by a housemaid.

Never on Saturday

THE traditional Saturday morning lessons at the King's School were scrapped at the start of the autumn term.

Serious road accident

THREE people were seriously injured when a pair of wheels from an articulated lorry spun off into the path of their car.

The car overturned and burst into flames on the A1 at Little Ponton.

Demolished

THE Spring Gardens foundry, built for Richard Hornsby before Queen Victoria was crowned, was demolished to make way for a London Road car showroom. It had been unused for more than 10 years.

Students' rag condemned for making mess of town

A FUN day organised by local students ended with residents complaining the town had been left looking like a barnyard.

Students from Kesteven College of Education, Stoke Rochford, paraded through the town with six floats to celebrate the end of their Rag Week.

The procession followed Welby Street, Wharf Road, High Street, Watergate, Brook Street and Castlegate. And there was no doubt of the route – it was littered with straw. A water and flour mix, which had been sprayed from containers, left council workmen clearing up until after midnight.

Borough surveyor Harry Haworth said: "We collected several lorry loads of straw. It was knee deep in places. We had to continue clearing up on Sunday. Students said some of their number had got over-excited.

But the occasion wasn't all bad news. Students raised £1,120 for charity.

Crowning glory for taxman

THE Crown building in Castlegate, a five-storey building which would bring together Government departments.

Work was nearing completion. These included the Inspector of Taxes, Collector of Taxes and Social Security. Until then, the departments had been scattered about the town, including Finkin Street, Castlegate and Spittlegate House.

Nearly 200 jobs go as tannery shuts

ONE hundred-and-eighty leather workers lost their jobs when Bjorlows closed.

Large amounts of money had been pumped into the Grantham tannery. A hike in the cost of hides and a company-wide shortage of skilled labour was blamed.

The Earlesfield Lane factory was owned by Barrow Hepburn Gale.

The tannery, originally Shaw's, had been there more than a century.

Chief executive Richard Odey said although a lot of money had been spent on improvements, the factory was too antiquated.

Maltings felled

THE former Pidcock's maltings, which ran the riverside length of Welham Street, was demolished despite preservation pleas by Grantham Civic Trust.

Owner John Wallwork claimed it was one of the ugliest buildings in Grantham. He planned to replace it with a three-storey car park

Jury calls for hospital to open X-ray department on Sundays

AN inquest jury called on Grantham Hospital to open its X-ray department on Sundays, following the death of a pensioner. The 80-year-old fell at Chandos House on a Sunday. Dr Eileen Gibb said he had a broken leg and booked an X-ray for the following day. A post-mortem examination revealed he also had broken his neck. He died of broncho-pneumonia due to the fractures.

Coroner John Pert recorded a verdict of accidental death.

Shop six days

GRANTHAM Chamber of Trade voted in favour of six-day trading in town. This saw the official end of early closing on Wednesdays.

The borough council endorsed their view.

1974 Grantham in the News

Blow for trades fair as gale rips into marquee

Greenwoods Row car park after the marquee blew down

THE trades fair turned out to be the best yet until gale force winds forced it to be abandoned. The high wind which finally blasted the giant marquee over was at noon on Saturday.

The fair, on Greenwoods Row car park, was plagued by winds all week. Officials were constantly on guard, watching and restoring poles and flapping canvasses. Inside the marquee on Saturday morning was described as 'eerie'. The wind howled and as the tops billowed and sagged alternately, unease grew.

When the Meteorological Office forecast even stronger winds, Chamber of Trade bosses decided to quit. There was a hasty withdrawal by visitors and exhibitors hurriedly removed stands.

A chamber spokesman said: "This is the ninth trades fair since the war and the first to end disappointingly.

"There were a lot of people yet to come." When the exhibition was called off, a record 9,000 people had already visited.

John strikes gold

PARAPLEGIC sportsman John Chilcott returned home from the Commonwealth Games in New Zealand with a gold medal.

The 35-year-old of Wroxall Drive, Grantham, was in the basketball team which beat Australia 63-62 in the final at Dunedin.

John was paralysed from the waist down after breaking his back in a car crash 13 years earlier.

Rising fame

A NEW comedy series, Rising Damp, began on ITV. It was written by Grantham scriptwriter Eric Chappell.

Starring Leonard Rossiter and Richard Beckinsale, the series was based on Mr Chappell's West End play The Banana Box and set in a seedy boarding house.

Although he had written several plays, this was Mr Chappell's breakthrough into television.

He was working on a new drama series, The Squirrels.

RAF camp reprieved

RAF Spitalgate, due to close this year, was reprieved.

Although the WRAF was transferred to Hereford, other sections including the Central Gliding School and Security Services (Central Region) were given a year to find a new home.

Police get ahead

LINCOLNSHIRE bobbies returned to wearing helmets.

Officers throughout the county said good bye to the peak cap with chequered band.

The force had stopped wearing helmets in June 1970 because of increased mechanisation.

The students march up Avenue Road

Students teachers protest

STUDENT teachers from Kesteven College of Education, Stoke Rochford, boycotted lectures and went on a protest march through Grantham to the Guildhall for a meeting.

The 150-odd students shouted slogans and handed leaflets to passers-by. They were demanding a grant increase of £3.50 a week.

Villagers shell-shocked

LONG Bennington villagers said they were frightened by soldiers on manouevres in their area.

They were awoken at dawn by rockets, flares and the rumble of tanks and scout cars, which disappeared as quickly as they came.

Parish council Ted Fairhall said all he found was the barn where they slept overnight plus beer cans and other litter. speed limit.

Milkman missing

POLICE quizzed householders in Dudley Road, Grantham, after a milk float was found abandoned early one morning.

The driver was traced to a relative's home in the north of England.

Pets die in blaze

A DOG and a budgerigar died when fire raged through a council house in Shelley Avenue.

Neighbours rescued one of the sons who was in bed at the time.

Canal plan to cost £2.6 million

A FEASIBILITY study commissioned by Grantham Canal Restoration Society estimated reopening the canal would cost £2,600,000. This would include £200,000 in Lincolnshire, and the opening of a canal basin west of the A1 Grantham bypass.

A county council spokesman said: "The development of the basin should include a picnic area, car park and caravan and camping site.

"There should also be amenities for walking, angling and canoeing."

Melton Borough Council was against the scheme, saying it was too much money for a canal that went nowhere.

New soccer stadium

THE biggest revolution in sporting facilities was planned by Buckminster Estates.

Planning applications were made for a new ground for Grantham Cricket Club on land behind Buckminster Gardens.

This would leave Grantham FC as sole users of the London Road ground. The trust submitted two plans to South Kesteven District Council. One for the cricket club, included a new pavilion and parking. The other, for London Road, involved turning the pitch 90 degrees and developing a frontage with shops, offices and possibly flats.

Council shuts up shop after half a millennium

AFTER 511 years, Grantham no longer had a town council.

From April 1, Grantham was administered by the new South Kesteven District Council. The Mayor, Paul Jones (right), handed over the mace and silver seal to Ald Lloyd Ramsden (left), who accepted it into safe keeping on behalf of the Charter Trustees.

Mr Jones said: "Grantham has come a long way from a small market town straddling the Great North Road to a thriving town of 28,000 people."

Indoor pool evacuated as chlorine gas leaked

GRANTHAM'S indoor swimming pool, Union Street, was evacuated on a Saturday afternoon in July when a chlorine cylinder leaked.

Three youngsters were taken to hospital and released after treatment for chlorine poisoning. Others in the pool, mainly children, were vomiting but otherwise unharmed.

Swimmers had to grab their clothes and make an early exit, although there was no panic. At one stage, police considered evacuating Key Markets supermarket across the road, but a change of wind direction sent the gas cloud safely in the opposite direction.

The incident happened when a cylinder was changed on the pool's filtering system. It became detached and caused an escape of gas.
It was discovered by instructor Clive Seymour, a former policeman.

Massive antiques haul at countess's home

ANTIQUES worth more than £100,000 were stolen in a raid on the Harston home of Nancye, Countess of Yarborough. Thieves, described by police as very professional, stole 249 items including a collection of snuff boxes and a large quantity of silver.

Det Chief Insp Jim Strong, leading the investigation, said it was similar to a raid at Denton Manor earlier in the year, from where antiques valued at £17,000 were taken. Among the items stolen from the 20-room mansion was a collection of 129 snuff boxes, collected by the countess's ex-husband the fifth Earl. In 1945 they had been valued at more than £6,000.

The majority of the silverware was stamped with the family crest.

Jobless rise

UNEMPLOYMENT rose by 100 in April, bringing the total to 785.

This was 4.4 per cent of those available, made up of 598 men, 168 women, 7 boys and 12 girls.

Bays under threat

HOUSEHOLDERS in Highfield Terrace, Bridge End Road, Grantham, said they were under threat from heavy lorries.

Several of the bay-windowed dwellings were shattered by vehicles crashing into them as they descended Somerby Hill.

They demanded tougher enforcement of the 30mph

Rise at Kontak

TWO hundred shop floor workers at Kontak Manufacturing, returned to work with an extra £7 per week in their pay packets.

They had been on strike for just over a week.

Gate record smashed by Town in FA Cup

Delighted Grantham fans before the start of the match.

ON probably the greatest day in the club's history, Grantham went out of the FA Cup in the third round.

They fell to Second Division runaway leaders Middlesbrough, managed by Jack Charlton.

But the Wearside visitors did not have it all their own way. For 20 minutes they took a roasting and needed defiant saves by Northern Ireland keeper Jim Platt and a brace of goal-line clearances by sweeper Stuart Boam. Graeme Souness did not know which way to turn as Brent Horobin, Ernie Nixon, Bob Norris and Denis Benskin tore the Middlesbrough defence apart.

But there was no fairy tale ending. Two breakaway goals from David Mills and Dave Armstrong gave the visitors a place in the next round.

For Grantham, who reached the third round by beating Rochdale 5–3 away in a replay, there was one consolation. The record 6,573 home gate produced £3,221 receipts of which Grantham cleared £1,100.

School to shut

KNIPTON Primary School, which had two classrooms, one teacher and six pupils, was closed by Lincolnshire County Council.

A county spokesman said they were the most expensive pupils to educate in the county.

Bread queues as strike begins to bite

QUEUES formed outside private bakeries when the major bread-makers went on strike.

Small bakers normally supplied only 20 per cent of bread but the December strike for higher wages left them overstretched.

Most town bakers stepped up production to four times their usual output but loaves sold as soon as they hit the shelves.

One baker said: "Obviously we are doing all we can to help, but being only a few weeks from Christmas, it has made it difficult."

Grantham in the News 1975

Deluge forces people from their homes

SIXTEEN hours of continuous rain caused flooding throughout the Grantham area in March.

The district council's weather recording station in Wyndham Park showed 39.9mm of rain had fallen at that time. This compared with 31mm for the whole of December, last year's wettest month.

Emergency services were at full stretch as the River Witham and brooks throughout the district overflowed. Roads became swamped and impassable and sandbags were brought in to stem the rising waters.

Houses in Witham Place were flooded, ruining carpets and furniture.

Bailing out had little effect.

Residents were evacuated to the homes of their friends and relatives.

Others braved the floods and moved upstairs.

Mayor of Grantham, Elsie Davies and her daughter Maureen spend four hours helping Witham Place residents mop up.

There was also severe flooding at Gonerby Hill Foot where raw sewage reached people's back yards.

On the A1, Gonerby Moor roundabout was under 50cm of water.

Sedgebrook, Edenham and Aslackby were also flooded.

Demolition of Guildhall is on hold for now

CAMPAIGNERS calling for Grantham Guildhall to be demolished lost the day.

They said the 100-year-old building was an underused white elephant. District council chief executive Russell Cann said: "Unless the building is improved, modified and adapted to modern standards there is no reason to believe future use would increase."

He said money had to be spent, adding: "It would be wrong to seek demolition and more realistic to enhance and improve the building and make use of it for future years."

He said it would be best used as an art gallery or a museum.

Mr Cann added the long-term plan was to build new district council offices, including a council chamber, and money should not be wasted on the sessions hall behind the Guildhall.

Pay claim

FARMWORKERS were demanding a minimum wage of £40 per week.

They rejected an offer by the Agricultural Wages Board of £27.80.

They also called for the introduction of a sickness scheme for at least 13 weeks.

*A plea was made for plastic guards to be outlawed and for better braking systems on tractors.

Duke opposes ban

THE Duke of Rutland, president of the Belvoir Hunt attacked supporters of a bill to ban hare coursing.

His outburst came at the hunt's annual meeting at the Chequers Inn, Woolsthorpe-by-Belvoir.

He said the bill, due to go before Parliament, was against the gentry.

He said: "Those who are anti-hare coursing are anti-everything. We are being attacked politically and we must defeat this bill.

"We are not going to accept it."

Backing him, hunt chairman the Rev J M Ashley said: "Those trying to get the bill through Parliament are anti-coursing because they cannot indulge in the sport themselves.

"It is sour grapes that's all."

Headmaster's namesake is well stuffed

A GRANTHAM headmaster was given the bird by a pupil – in the nicest possible way.

Young taxidermist Adrian Walls (14) gave his St Hugh's School head the woodcock he had stuffed for his Duke of Edinburgh Award.

The bird was found by two schoolmates and it is believed it was killed flying into a closed window.

And the headmaster Mike Woodcock was chuffed to bits with the new trophy and proudly displayed it on his desk.

Fireworks in the streets

THE Fireworks Five, a five kilometre road race through the streets of Grantham was a great success.

The race is planned to be run in November each year. Picture shows the race running up East Street, past the Fine Fare car park.

Evicted family put in rat-infested home

A HOMELESS Grantham family were rehoused by South Kesteven District Council in a two-bedroomed house in Witham Terrace scheduled for demolition.

All but three houses were vacant.

They were evicted from Welland Court because of rent arrears.

The house was home to a woman, her partner, three children aged 11, 10 and four and her eldest daughter and partner with their three-week-old baby.

The woman said: "The house is not fit to bring children up in.

"It is riddled with woodworm, the woodwork is rotten.

"We have had rats and mice, ants and a plague of hopping fleas.

"Because of the damp, my furniture, clothing and carpets have been ruined." She said vandals were a further problem. A lighted paper had been pushed through their letter box and the TV aerial cut.

She said: "As well as paying off the arrears, I'm paying £2.85 a week on this place." A council spokesman said no other properties were available.

Council houses on Earlesfield cost more than stately homes

COUNCIL houses cost more each than a stately home, members of the district council were told.

Treasurer Bill Cooke said the 114 homes being built on Earlesfield estate would cost £966,000 including £50,000 fees and £8,000 for land.

He said: "The figure we are tendering bears no resemblance to the actual cost. The annual loan charges over the proposed 60 years amounts to £110,000.

"That is £1,018 a year for every house or more than £60,000 altogether for a house which cost less than £8,500 to build."

Bogus vicar stole children's cash

A BANKRUPT publishing company editor toured the country posing as a parson while on the run from prison. But his three months of freedom came to an end when he stole the charity collection bottle from a Grantham pub.

Claiming to be a lecturer at Lincoln Theological College, the 40-year-old alcoholic lived a life of luxury in hotels, then left without paying. But his luck ran out when he tried to steal £16 in a charity bottle from the Blue Pig, Vine Street.

Landlady Lil Smith spotted the bottle, containing cash for Dr Frier's Crippled Children Holiday Fund had gone and went around the town with police to find him.

He also left the George Hotel owing £8.38 for accommodation and stole a quilt cover worth £8.75 from Marks & Spencer.

He asked for six other offences to be considered.

He was already serving three years for previous crimes.

He was transferred to Lincoln Crown Court for sentencing.

He had been at large since December 1974 after walking out of Sudbury open prison, Suffolk.

Well, well. Where did my garden go?

A NORTON Street resident had the shock of his life when he looked out of his bedroom window to admire his garden. Half of it had disappeared.

In its place was a three metre square hole, about four metres deep.

A communal well, last used 30 years previously, had collapsed.

The resident, who remained anonymous, said: "Maybe I'll be able to have a swimming pool. "It's just about the right depth."

Last post

WELBY sub-postmistress Evelyn Baxter retired after 70 years behind the counter.

She had held the position since 1928, but first worked there in 1904, a year before she was allowed to.

She was a Sunday school teacher for 55 years and ran its annual outing for half-a-century.

Business booming

KONTAK Manufacturing was bursting at the seams.

Order books were so full, they agreed to take over a modern factory on the site of the former Bjorlow tannery making way for 60 more jobs.

Development at the Londonthorpe Lane works was set to continue, adding a further 140 to the payroll.

Bargain home

LITTLE Ponton House, an eight-bedroomed village house set in 1.07 acres, was on the market at £25,000.

Epiphany Church dedicated

THE Church of the Epiphany, was dedicated by Bishop of Grantham the Rt Rev Dennis Hawker and Canon Graham Sansbury, Rector of Grantham.

The Church, on The Grove, to serve Earlesfield, took only three months to build.

Workmen are pictured hanging the bell, which formerly came from Little Humby Chapel.

In the background is St Hugh's School.

Slump in gates

THE average league gate at Grantham FC's London Road ground had been 897, the lowest since the 1962-63 season, a stormy club annual meeting was told.

It was also the first time in 10 years, the average was less than four figures.

Wedged under bridge

A MIDLAND Red bus destined for Leicester only got as far as Harlaxton Road railway bridge.

It became firmly wedged under the bridge and was too badly damaged to continue its journey.

Court in the act

BURGLARS who broke into Grantham courthouse, London Road, left empty-handed.

After scaling a drainpipe and breaking in through the ceiling, they set fire to documents in the general office causing damage put at £500.

Court clerk David Holmes said: "Someone must have had a grudge."

Closure causes chaos

THE closure of Belton Lane bridge over the Witham caused traffic mayhem. A Bailey bridge was installed while essential repairs were carried out.

Belmont school opens

BELMONT County Primary School, Harrowby Lane, opened its doors to children for the first time. The first phase was to admit 120 pupils but the school was expected to hold 280 by the end of phase two.

Dangerous games

AN area where children played regularly had six open manholes.

They were on open waste ground running alongside the railway station.

Each had a drop of seven metres but none had covers.

Girls build boat

PUPILS at Walton Girls' School built themselves a boat after being introduced to the joys of sailing.

Handy Craft, Mirror class dinghy 46809, joined the fleet at North Hykeham where they resumed sailing in summer.

The girls spent an afternoon each week at the Grantham Teachers' Centre, Castlegate.

Headteacher Mrs Isaacs said: "The girls took to boat-building like ducks to water."

Maggie's the boss

GRANTHAM-born Margaret Thatcher was set to become Britain's first woman Prime Minister when she won the leadership of the Conservative Party.

Her father, Alfred Roberts was a councillor, alderman and mayor of the town.

Short staffed

GRANTHAM Hospital was having to transfer patients to Nottingham and Lincoln because of staffing problems.

Staff levels were so tight, they were unable to operate when someone went on holiday.

Youngsters on rampage

TEENAGERS in the Cherry Orchard area were accused of being out of control.

Coun Fred Burrows said: "They are going into gardens ripping down trees.

"They even locked a 70-year-old lady in her garden shed."

Wartime shell found in the Witham bank

A LIVE, wartime armour-piercing shell was found by a man clearing up a stretch of the Witham at the bottom of his garden.

Peter Angel, of Dudley Road, was clearing up the weeds in the river and bank when he made the discovery.

Bomb disposal experts recovered it and took it to Ropsley quarry where it was detonated.

Mr Angel, a welder at Aveling Barford, said: "It was covered in slime and at first I though it was a milk bottle.

"It weighed about 40-lb and I thought it might be a bomb."

Two Army sergeants arrived and wanted to blow it up there but changed their minds when they realised the blast would have broken a lot of windows.

Mr Angel said: "It's a mystery how it got there."